Embrace CHANGE for SUCCESS

Dale Carnegie Success Series titles
published by Manjul Publishing House

- *Living an Enriched Life*
- *Become an Effective Leader*
- *How to Jump-Start Your (Next) Career*
- *10 Steps to a More Fulfilling Life*
- *Overcoming Worry & Stress*
- *Communicating Your Way to Success*
- *How to Have Rewarding Relationships, Win Trust and Influence People*
- *Life Is Short, Make It Great!*
- *Resolve Conflicts in Your Life*

Embrace CHANGE for SUCCESS

DALE CARNEGIE

MANJUL

Manjul Publishing House

First published in India by

MANJUL

Manjul Publishing House

•7/32, Ansari Road, Daryaganj, New Delhi 110 002 - India
Website: www.manjulindia.com

Registered Office:
•10, Nishat Colony, Bhopal 462 003 - India

The Success Series:
Embrace Change for Success

This edition first published in India in 2018

ISBN 978-93-87383-52-4

Cover Design by Trinankur Banerjee

Printed and bound in India by Thomson Press (India) Ltd.

CONTENTS

Preface

Success in one's career is dynamic—not static. Whether our goal is to maintain current success, build continuing success, or move up to even greater success, we must not only be willing to accept change, but to be alert to when we should initiate it.

Too often people feel that as their methods and systems are good and sound, they need not be changed. "If it's not broken, don't fix it." Unfortunately, this is adage is not always true. What worked well in the past may not be the best approach for the present or the future. No matter how good what we are doing may be, today changes in circumstances may signal a need to do things differently.

Whether it is on the job or in our personal lives, if we want to make progress, we must be willing to make changes—often major changes—in the way we do our jobs or even live our lives.

In this book, we will look at the reasons why we often resist change and the steps we can take to overcome this resistance. Examples will be drawn from both personal and job-related situations.

This does not mean that we assume everything we do needs to change, but it does mean that we should be open to new ideas.

The need to change may be required because of new technologies. The move into computerization is a major example of the need to reexamine all operations and adapt to the new technology. Sometimes the need to change is caused by economic factors. When demand for a company's products or services declines, changes in their systems, methods, or structure may be essential for their survival. When the economy surges, on the other hand, other changes need be made to meet new demands.

Changes may be mandated by changes in the laws of the country or state in which an organization is located. Laws prohibiting discrimination due to race, religion, national origin, sex, age, and other factors have required major changes in human resources policies and practices.

We will examine various aspects of change and provide suggestions on how we can make these changes help us on the road to success in our endeavors.

Among the areas covered are:

- Changes as a step toward success
- Adjusting to change
- How and when we should suggest or initiate change
- How to deal with change as part of a team
- Reducing stress when dealing with change
- Adjusting to working with people of diverse cultures
- The gender and generational gaps in the workplace

Reading this book is the first step in coping with change. To get the most out of this book, read all of it first to absorb the overall concept of making change work for you. Then reread each chapter to start applying the guidelines for achieving each of the areas covered. This will start you on the track that has helped men and women in all careers to accept, adjust to, and often initiate changes that enabled their organizations to not only survive, but thrive, resulting in the acceleration of their own progress to success.

Arthur R. Pell, Ph.D.
Editor

1

THE "S" SUCCESS FACTORS

The key to success is our ability to adapt.

Peter Drucker

Most people hope for success in their jobs and indeed, in all aspects of their lives. Their ideas of success may differ, but they all agree upon the desirability of its attainment.

Attainment—that word embodies the essence of what we call success. It is the getting-there idea—reaching our goal.

Many people have tried to show the way to success, and while some have rendered valuable service to those who were following them, none have yet been able to tell the whole story. The reason is obvious: no two temperaments are exactly alike; nature delights in variety. No two sets of circumstances are precisely the same, and so it would be folly to attempt to lay down rules of universal application that would lead all to the great goal of success. One has but to look around to see the different needs of individuals in order to see that this is true. Each and every person who has succeeded has done so in a different way—generally along some original lines of action. In fact, the quality of individuality plays the most important role in success. Strong individuality allows people to depart from any set rules or laid-out courses of action. And so, it may be stated as a general principle that all people must work out their own success along the lines of their own individuality, rather than by following any set rule or line of conduct. But close examination of men and women who have achieved notable success can give us some useful clues that can be applied in our own lives.

There are probably as many approaches to success as there are successful people, yet by analyzing the histories of successful people, we find there are many qualities they have in common. As all of these begin with the letter "S," we refer to them as the "S" factors.

1. Self-Confidence

The primary ingredient of success is self-confidence. This term is self-explanatory—it means that to achieve success we must believe in ourselves. However, this does not mean that we have no weaknesses. It means that we are to take inventory of ourselves, find out what qualities we have that are strong and useful, and then organize these qualities into a definite plan of action with which to attain the object of our definite goal.

Self-confident people never lose faith in their ability to face and cope with their fears. There is an old story about a boy who was afraid of the big bully in his school. One day his grandmother gave him a talisman that she assured him his grandfather had carried during a war and which, she said, had the property of making its owner invincible. Nothing could hurt him, she told him, while he wore this talisman. Nothing could stand up against him. He believed her. Then the next time the bully of the town started to beat him up, he wiped up the earth with him. And that was only the start. Before the year was out he had a reputation as the most daring soul in the community.

A few days later, when his grandmother felt that he was thoroughly cured, she told him the truth—that the "talisman" was merely a piece of old junk she'd picked up from a roadside shop—that she knew all he needed was faith in himself—belief that he could do these things.

It is our own belief in ourselves that counts. It is the consciousness of dominant power within us that makes all things attainable. We can do anything we think we can. This knowledge is literally the gift of the gods, for through it we can solve every human problem. It should make each of us an incurable optimist. It is the open door to faring well. Keep that door open—by expecting to gain everything that is right.

We are entitled to every good thing. Therefore, expect nothing but good. Defeat does not need to follow victory. No limitation rests upon us. So don't let any enter your lives.

To succeed, we must have faith in our own ability to do whatever we make up our mind to do. We must also cultivate the habit of faith in those who are associated with us, whether they are in a position of authority over us, or we over them.

A definite, chief aim is the starting point of all noteworthy achievement, but self-confidence is the unseen force that coaxes, drives, or leads us on and on until the object of the aim is a reality. Without self-confidence no achievements would ever get beyond the "aim" stage and mere aims, within themselves, are worth nothing. Many people have vague sorts of aims, but they are afraid of failure. All of us have had successes and failures. People who dwell on their failures are doomed to repeat these failures. People who concentrate on their achievements will build up strong positive attitudes, which will solidify their confidence. Shakespeare said, "What is past is prologue." Every aspect of our past influences our future, but we can choose those past experiences that we wish to let dominate our thinking. We must make an effort to learn from our failures, and then write them off once the lesson is learned. Let the successes in our past be the pre-determinants of our future.

People who do great things are powerful in their affirmations. They have tremendous positive ability; they do not know the meaning of negatives. Their power of assertion and their conviction of ability to do anything are so strong that the opposite does not occur to them. When they make up their minds to do a thing, they take it for granted that they can do it. They are not filled with doubts and fears, no matter how people may scoff. Indeed, nearly all the great men and women who have pushed progress along have been called dreamers. Yet, we owe the blessings of modern civilization to the sublime self-confidence of such men and women and that indomitable faith in their mission, which nothing could shake. What if Copernicus and Galileo had given up when they were denounced as insane? Science of today is built on their unshaken confidence that the world is round and that the earth moves around the sun instead of the sun around it! Throughout all history, the great teachers, philosophers and prophets have disagreed with one another on many different things. But on this one point they are in complete and unanimous agreement. Listen to what Marcus Aurelius, the great Roman emperor said, "A man's life is what his thoughts make of it."

Another great thinker and writer who also served as the Prime Minister of the United Kingdom on two occasions, Benjamin Disraeli said, "Everything comes if a man will only wait. I have brought myself by long meditation to the conviction that a human being with a settled purpose must accomplish it and that nothing can resist a will that will stake even existence for its fulfillment."

Ralph Waldo Emerson said, "A man is what he thinks about all day long." William James said, "The greatest discovery of my generation is that human beings can alter their lives by altering their attitudes of mind."

And he also said, "We need only in cold blood act as if the thing in question were real and it will become infallibly real by growing into such a connection with our life, that it will become real. It will become so knit with habit and emotion that our interests in it will be those which characterize belief." He also said,

> *"If you only care enough for a result, you will almost certainly attain it. If you wish to be rich, you will be rich. If you wish to be learned, you will be learned. If you wish to be good, you will be good. Only you*

must then really wish these things, and wish them exclusively, and not wish at the same time a hundred other incompatible things just as strongly."

Dr Norman Vincent Peale said,

"This is one of the greatest laws in the universe. Fervently do I wish I had discovered it as a very young man. It dawned upon me much later in life, and I found it to be one of the greatest, if not my greatest discovery outside of my relationship to God. And the great law briefly and simply stated is that if we think in negative terms, we get negative results. If we think in positive terms, we will achieve positive results."

2. Self-Discipline

Arthur Rubenstein, one of the greatest pianists of his time, attributed much of his success to his ability to set a practice schedule and stick to it. Even though he had achieved fame and wealth, he continued to practice daily throughout his long career. Most great people did not have to be pushed by a boss to get their job done. They were able to discipline themselves to do what they had to do without external pressures. Champion athletes work out for hours each day to keep in shape. Self-discipline starts with a commitment to achieve and then make the necessary sacrifices to assure that the commitment will be met.

We can become superb performers by disciplining ourselves to become technically proficient, by never ceasing to train, by teaching others, and by thinking carefully and thoroughly before we begin.

In a complex operation, a lot of time must often be given to the planning and to the work itself. Before making a sales call, the successful sales representative thinks carefully about all of the possible problems that may develop and how they can be handled. Executives think about every ramification any of their decisions may cause before making any decision. This is also true when it comes to the top performers in the theater, cinema, television or in sports.

One aspect of self-discipline is the ability to control one's emotions and actions. Lack of self-control has brought grief to more people than any other shortcoming known to the human race. This evil shows itself, at one time or another, in every person's life.

Self-discipline requires us to turn our attention upon each detail of everyday work. We must pour all our thought into this piece of work until we can do it to perfection and with joy. As long as we have irksome tasks or "drudgery," we may rest assured it is because we have not yet put in enough thought.

This is the finest "concentration" practice in the world—just to put our whole soul into the one thing we are doing. When we have used this practice long enough we will do it beautifully and with joy.

About this time we will find our thought-force has flowed into our work and filled it with energy. We will take happy little mental flights away from our work; little inspirations will come to us, and always our thoughts will come back to our work with joy.

Suppose our work just now is "five-finger exercises"—learning to use our fingers. If we put all our thought into each movement, we will make each accurately. When this happens the thought flows, or overflows, in beautiful fancies that the fingers are ready to express. And all is pleasure. If we let our mind wander ever so slightly, our fingers follow. Our exercises will be slovenly because our thought is divided, and we haven't sufficient strength of mind to bear dividing. If we practice with a divided mind it will take us five times as long to accomplish the art of using our fingers, and we will never use them to the best advantage.

Do we see now what concentration upon daily tasks is for? To fill each part of our body with loving intelligence in expressing thought. The everyday tasks given to us in the school of life are the "scales" and "five-finger exercises" that we must put our soul into mastering before that soul can express anything more beautiful in the way of life-symphonies.

As Steve Jobs said,

> *"Your work is going to fill a large part of your life, and the only way to be truly satisfied is to do what you believe is great work. And the only way to do great work is to love what you do. If you haven't found it yet, keep looking. Don't settle. As with all matters of the heart, you'll know when you find it. And, like any great relationship, it just gets better and better as the years roll on. So keep looking until you find it. Don't settle."*

3. Spurred On

Successful people are continually spurred on to succeed. They do not need external motivation, such as an immediate reward, to motivate them. They become so enthusiastic about their work that they cannot wait to get at it every morning and hate to stop at the end of the workday. Their energy seems unlimited. When problems develop, they are not discouraged. Indeed, the problem becomes an additional spur to excite them even more.

In the nonstop round-the-world flight of the Voyager, the plane's designer, Burt Ruton and the pilots, Dick Ruton and Jeanna Yeager, met rejection and failure all along the way, but their enthusiasm and commitment to the project helped them overcome the problems and generated renewed energies that led to their success.

The first step in spurring ourselves on is to have a definite goal toward which to work. We must have definite plans for attaining any goal. Nothing is ever accomplished that is worthwhile without a definite plan of procedure that is systematically and continuously followed day-by-day. For how could we hope to succeed, or how could we know when success had been reached, if the nature of the accomplishment—the goal—had never been determined?

To cultivate the imagination so it will eventually suggest ideas on its own initiative, we should make it our business to keep a record of all the useful, ingenious, and practical ideas we see in the work we and our associates are doing. However, we must keep a broad focus and also look at what is being done in other lines of work outside of our own occupation. Make a practice of cataloguing every idea, concept, or thought that we observe or that occurs to us that is capable of practical use, and then take these ideas and work them into new plans. Today most people do this by using appropriate applications on their Blackberry, iPad, or similar device. However, some people are more comfortable just jotting them down in an ordinary, pocket-sized notebook.

When a problem develops or a new situation arises, we refer to our notes and assemble this knowledge into new combinations, and come up with adaptations or brand-new ideas to deal with the matter.

Barry, a mid-level technician in his company, often dreamed up good (and sometimes brilliant) ideas, but he never took steps to implement them or even to pass them on to his management. As a result, he never moved ahead in his job. He was perceived as a mediocre employee who did his job well, but not superbly. Had Barry converted his dreams into action, he might have moved far ahead in his career.

> *The greatest crime in the world is not developing your potential. When you do what you do best, you are helping not only yourself, but the world.*
>
> Roger Williams

Nothing spurs us on more effectively than being enthusiatic about what we are doing. The true meaning of "enthusiasm" gives this quality an importance that far surpasses the cheerleading attitude that this word too often brings to mind. Rooted in the Greek, it means "inspired" and literally means "the God within us." Those who come by it naturally are fortunate indeed.

Enthusiasm is a driving force that not only gives greater power to the one who has it, but is contagious and affects all whom it reaches. Enthusiasm over the work in which one is engaged takes the drudgery out of that work. It has been observed that even laborers engaged in the toilsome job of ditch digging can take the drabness out of their work by singing.

Flaming enthusiasm, backed up by horse sense and persistence, is the quality that most frequently makes for success.

Dale Carnegie

It is a well-known fact that people succeed most readily when engaged in an occupation that they like best, and for this reason they readily become enthusiastic over such a career. Enthusiasm is also the basis of creative imagination. When the mind is vibrating at a high rate, it is receptive to similar high rates of vibration from outside sources, thus providing a favorable condition for creative imagination. It can be observed that enthusiasm plays an important part in other principles constituting the law of success philosophy, namely, accurate thought and a pleasant personality.

4. Self-Starter

Welcome every morning with a smile. Look on the new day as another golden opportunity to complete what you were unable to finish yesterday. Be a self-starter. Let your first hour set the theme of success and positive action that is certain to echo through your entire day. Today will never happen again. Don't waste it with a false start or no start at all. You were not born to fail.

Og Mandino

Some people are like cellphones. In order to get them started, they have to be charged up. Such people are less likely to be achievers than those who can start anytime by pushing their inner self-starter.

For instance, John and Bill started work the same day and spent their entire careers with the same company. At the time of their retirement, John was the supervisor of a small department and Bill was an executive vice president. John could never understand why he had made so little progress. He often said, "I've always done what they asked me to do, and I did it well." Bill knew why he had always done so well. From the beginning of his career, he initiated projects, made suggestions, took the ball and ran with it without having to be told to do so.

To be a successful self-starter we must establish for ourselves a set of principles that will guide us in the way we work. How do people begin the building of a house? They first get a blueprint of the proposed edifice, and then proceed to build according to the plan, scrupulously following it in every detail, beginning with the foundation. Should they neglect the foundation, their labor would be wasted, and their building, should it reach completion without tumbling to pieces, would be insecure and worthless. The same law holds good in any important work—the right beginning and first essential is a definite mental plan on which to build.

The following four basic principles are key factors in starting a project:

- *Concentration.* Concentration means undivided attention to the matter in hand, intelligent focus of the mind on the work to be done—it includes all that is meant by thoroughness, exactness, and efficiency.

- *Honesty.* Honesty involves the absence of all trickery, lying, and deception by word, look or gesture. It includes sincerity, saying what we mean, and meaning what we say. It scorns obsequiousness. It builds up good reputations, and good reputations build up good businesses.
- *Economy.* Economy means the husbanding of one's physical vitality and mental resources. It demands the conservation of energy by the avoidance of debilitating self-indulgences and sensual habits. It holds for its followers strength, endurance, vigilance and the capacity to achieve.
- *Generosity.* Generosity is more than giving money. There is a giving of thoughts, deeds and sympathy, the bestowing of goodwill, and being generous toward opponents.

Commit to Achievement

Self-starters commit themselves to succeed in accomplishing their goals. Commitment is more than just making a resolution.

Every year on New Year's Day, millions of resolutions are made. People promise themselves they will lose weight, stop smoking, learn a foreign language, be nicer to their parents or children, or make some substantial improvement in their jobs or in their personal lives. How many of these resolutions are ever carried out?

Resolutions are not limited to New Year's day. All of us, from time to time, decide that we will accomplish something important to us—even start to work on it—but in a short time it is forgotten.

Paul Peters resolved to go on a strict diet to lose some weight. He commenced the diet with great enthusiasm and carefully chose his menus. However, his job called for frequent business lunches and dinners. On these occasions he neglected the diet completely. When he saw he was not losing the weight as rapidly as he had hoped, he gave up.

When Lisa Grant's boss announced that the company was going to install a new computer system, he offered anybody who wished to learn the system an opportunity to enroll in a training program. This could give them much greater growth potential in the company. Lisa registered for the course and attended the first two classes. When the program began to get more difficult, Lisa found excuses for not attending and eventually dropped out.

Assuming that Paul really wanted to lose weight and Lisa was truly sincere in her desire to learn the new computer, what could they have done to assure that they would meet their goals—even when it became tougher than they thought it would be?

In order to assure that a goal will be met, we have to commit ourselves to achieving it. Commitment is more than just making a resolution. It is a solemn pledge that we will do all that we can. It cannot be taken lightly. If we follow these guidelines, there is a much greater chance that we will succeed.

> *Always bear in mind that your own resolution to succeed is more important than any other.*
>
> Abraham Lincoln

Set a Clear and Specific Final Goal

Instead of saying "I want to lose weight," set the exact number of pounds you wish to lose. In this way you can keep score and see day by day how close you are to reaching that goal. When the goal cannot be quantified, make your targets as specific as we can: "Be able to order a meal in French," or "Give a talk to my professional association."

Set Intermediate Goals

"My overall goal is to swim thirty laps in fifteen minutes. By the end of the third week, I should be swimming thirty laps in twenty minutes." "The deadline for my report is March 30. By March 10, I will have completed all the preliminary research and by March 20, I will have the statistical analysis completed."

By setting intermediate goals, we make it easier to accomplish our overall goal. Take things one step at a time. Instead of worrying about losing twenty pounds, we think in terms of losing only five pounds and when that is accomplished work on the next five pounds and so on.

It also helps us establish control points. These are critical steps along the way by which we can measure how well we are doing. In school, these control points may be quarterly or mid-term exams. On a job, they may be periodic performance reviews. In our commitment to achievement, we must set our own control points to examine what has or has not been accomplished. If the intermediate goals have been reached at that point, it reinforces our commitment to continue. If we have not made as much progress as planned, it enables us to determine what steps we can now take to get back on track.

Make a Contract

A contract is a binding agreement. When financial problems compelled Rocco Esposito to leave college after his sophomore year, he made a commitment that he would get his degree within five years. He knew this meant taking night and weekend courses, spending a significant portion of his earnings on his education and sacrificing most social and recreational aspects of his life. To assure that he would do this, he drew up a written contract with himself outlining his long-term goal—to obtain his degree and the intermediate goals—courses to be taken and when he expected to complete them. When difficulties arose or he was tempted to slacken, he would reread his contract and renew his commitment.

Share the Aim With Another Person

The great writer on self-motivation, Napoleon Hill, recommended that we share our commitments with another person. Rocco gave a copy of his contract to his brother, Joe, who signed the contract as a witness and promised that he would see that Rocco lived up to it. Over the next few years when, due to the pressure of the heavy load of work and school, Rocco was tempted to drop courses, the support he received from Joe helped him keep his commitment.

Selecting the person or persons with whom we can share our commitment is important. It must be somebody we respect and do not want to disappoint. This person must be as enthusiastic about our reaching our goal as we are. If the goal is personal, it could be our spouse, a family member, or close friend. In a business situation, we can share our commitment with our mentor, a close colleague, a fellow-member of a professional association or even our boss, if a good relationship exists.

Give Ourselves a Reward

When we have accomplished our goal, we should receive a significant reward. From whom? Ourselves, of course. Max had quit smoking a dozen times but he always started again within a few months. He made a commitment to stop permanently and promised himself that if he kept his commitment for one full year, he would buy the big flat screen TV that he'd always desired. By saving the money formerly spent on cigarettes, at the end of the year he had enough for the television.

Knowing that they will give themselves a tangible reward in addition to the psychic satisfaction of meeting the goal helps some people adhere to their goals.

To achieve what we desire in life requires real commitment. By setting goals that are clear and specific, establishing control points so we can measure progress, making a contract with ourselves and sharing it with someone we respect, and rewarding ourselves when the objective is achieved, we will reach the goals that are important to us in our jobs and in every other aspect of our lives.

5. Sensitivity

With few exceptions, most achievement involves working with other people. Empathy—the ability to put ourselves mentally in the other person's shoes—is essential to success. Managers must be sensitive to the feelings of those they supervise; sales representatives must be sensitive to the reactions of their customers; elected officials must be sensitive to the needs of their constituents.

Two of Dale Carnegie's principles of effective human relations are:

"Become genuinely interested in other people," and "Try honestly to see things from the other person's point of view."

By applying these principles to our daily interactions with the people at our workplace and in our personal life, we will encourage them to do their best and that in turn will help us do our best.

Cultivate a Love of People

When our greatest desire is to make others happy, when this desire becomes an enduring passion for serving others, we will be driven to do everything necessary for success.

In short, only those passionately devoted to giving more or better service, and passionately devoted to always serving more people, can ordinarily expect success, and such devotion can best be inspired by love for the people to whom the service is rendered.

This desire to serve others is an emotion that is without danger to our mental well-being, that is in harmony with every law of God and humankind, that can subordinate conflicting feelings that otherwise lead to inefficiency, and that will supply the driving force necessary to long-continued application and inspired effort.

As with the other rules, let us weigh this one and see if it is confirmed by the histories of successful people. Consider, for example, a typical case of two singers. Both have a talent for singing popular songs; both have equally good voices for this purpose, though they have poor voices from the viewpoint of a musical critic. With their mediocre talents, neither should ordinarily be expected to make a success.

One singer never gets anywhere. He sings chiefly to suit himself. He desires success, but does not love his audiences. His first thought is to show what a fine singer he is. The audiences sense his attitude and give him a frigid hearing. His failure is complete and final. The other singer loves his audiences. His foremost thought is to make them happy. He sings the songs they like in the way they like them. In his desire to increase the happiness of his audiences, he is forever and keenly studying them. He notices immediately if any one of his mannerisms pleases or displeases. He is constantly trying to determine from individual acquaintances and from different audiences what types of singing is most pleasing to people. He mingles with people all the time; first, because he loves them; second, to learn their likes and dislikes in the matter of singing. He may starve for years, while he is learning what his beloved people like, but nothing can discourage him. After years of trial and error, of love so great that he cannot give up, the audiences begin to recognize his love for them. They begin to listen with respect, eagerness, and delight. Here, they think, is a man like us, he knows us and is one of us; he knows what we like. He likes us, therefore, we like him. There is a warmth of feeling in his songs which other singers lack, as far as his kind of audiences are concerned. Suddenly this singer becomes famous.

In the above example, we could substitute two actors for the two singers, two writers of plays or novels, two builders of homes, two restaurant owners, two gas-station owners, two retailers, two manufacturers, two salespeople, two preachers, two lawyers, two physicians, or almost two of anything else. The successes are usually for those who love their public or their clientele and are passionately devoted, therefore, to giving better service or to making their clientele happy.

It must not be thought that love for people can be cultivated only through social activities. It can be strengthened in the ordinary contacts of our business or employment. Retailers mingle with the customers in their stores, executives with their employees, salespeople with prospects and customers. Through constant association, they learn to love their clientele, to enjoy making people happy through their service, and, if they are to be a success, to devote themselves passionately to finding ways and means by which ever-increasing numbers may likewise be made happy.

> *Develop success from failures. Discouragement and failure are two of the surest stepping-stones to success.*
>
> Dale Carnegie

Cultivate an Attitude of Tolerance

Intolerance has caused more grief than any of the many other forms of ignorance. Practically all wars grow out of intolerance. Misunderstandings between management and labor are usually the outgrowth of intolerance.

It is impossible for any person to observe the law on accurate thought without having first acquired the habit of tolerance. The most damaging form of intolerance grows out of religious and racial differences of opinion. Civilization, as we know it today, bears the deep wounds of gross intolerance all through the ages, mostly those of a religious nature. Whether we are good neighbors or bad depends largely on how tolerant we are with one another.

Intolerance is the result of ignorance or, stated conversely, the lack of knowledge. Well-informed people are seldom intolerant, because they know that no one knows enough to be entitled to judge others.

There are many reasons why one should be tolerant, the chief of them being the fact that tolerance permits cool reason to guide one in the direction of facts, and this, in turn, leads to accurate thinking. Those whose minds have been closed by intolerance, no matter of what brand or nature, can never become accurate thinkers, which is sufficient reason to cause us to master intolerance.

It may not be our duty to be tolerant with other people whose ideas, religious views, politics, and racial tendencies are different from ours, but it is our privilege! We do not have to ask permission from anyone to be tolerant; this is something that we control, in our own minds, therefore, the responsibility that goes with the choice is also our own.

Intolerance closes the doorway to opportunity in a thousand ways and shuts out the light of intelligence. The moment we open our mind to facts, and take the attitude that the last word is seldom said on any subject and that there always remains the chance that still more truth may be learned, we begin to know the law of tolerance. If we practice this habit for long we will soon become thinkers, with the ability to solve the problems that confront us in our struggle to make a place for ourselves in our chosen field or endeavor.

Success is simple. Do what's right, the right way, at the right time.

Arnold H Glasow

Using the Golden Rule to Win Cooperation

The golden rule—do unto others as you would have them do unto you—is one of in some ways, the most important laws of success. Despite the fact that for more than five thousand years the great philosophers have all taught the law of the golden rule, the great majority of people of today look upon it as a sort of pretty text for preachers to build sermons on.

The golden rule philosophy is the real basis on which children should be governed. It is also the real basis on which adults should be managed. Through force, or by taking advantage of unfair circumstances, one may build a fortune without observing the golden rule, and many do this, but such fortunes cannot bring happiness. Ill-gotten gain is bound to destroy the peace of mind of all.

Ideas are the most valuable products of the human mind. If we can create usable ideas and put them to work, we can do whatever we want. Wealth created or acquired by the golden rule philosophy does not bring with it a flock of regrets, nor does it disturb the conscience and destroy the peace of mind.

Fortunate are they who make the golden rule their business or professional slogan and then live by it faithfully, both literally and figuratively.

In truth, the golden rule philosophy is based upon a powerful law which, when understood and faithfully practiced, will enable anyone to get others to cooperate with him or her. It is a well-known truth that most people follow the practice of returning good or evil, act for act. If we slander anyone, we will be slandered in return. If we praise anyone, we will be praised. If we favor someone in business, we will be favored in return.

There are exceptions to this rule, of course, but by and large the law works out. Like attracts like. This is in accordance with a great natural law, and it works in every particle of matter and in every form of energy in the universe. The successful attract the successful. Failures attract failures.

Doing More Than Paid For

The law of the golden rule is closely related to the law on the habit of doing more than paid for. By rendering more service than we are paid to render, encourages others to do more for us than required. This is the basis of the golden rule philosophy.

There is no escape from the fact that those who render more service than they're paid to render eventually will be eagerly sought by those who will be willing to pay for more than is actually done. Compound interest on compound interest is nature's rate, when she goes to pay the indebtedness incurred through application of this law.

This law is so fundamental, so obvious, yet so simple. It is one of the great mysteries of human nature that it is not more generally understood and practiced. Behind its use lie possibilities that stagger the imagination of the most visionary person. Through its use may one learn the real secret—all the secret there is—about the art of getting others to do that which we wish them to do.

If we want a favor from someone, make it our business to seek out the person from whom we want the favor and, in an appropriate manner, render that person an equivalent of the favor we wish from him or her. If he or she does not respond at first, double the dose and render him or her another favor, and another, and another, and so on, until finally the person will, out of shame if nothing more, come back and render us a favor.

We get others to cooperate with us by first cooperating with them!

The foregoing sentence is worth reading a hundred times, for it contains the gist of one of the most powerful laws available to those with the intention of attaining great success. It may sometimes happen, and it will, that the particular individual to whom we render useful service will never render us a similar services. But keep this important truth in mind that even though one person fails to respond, someone else will observe the transaction and, out of a desire to see justice done, or perhaps with a more selfish motive in mind, will render us the service to which we are entitled.

Whatsoever a man soweth, that shall he also reap!

Galatians 6:7

The above quote fom the Bible is more than a mere exhortation; it is a great practical truth that may be made the foundation of every successful achievement. From winding pathways or straight, every thought we send out, every deed we perform, will gather a flock of other thoughts or deeds according to its own nature, and come back to us in due time.

There is no escape from this truth. It is as eternal as the universe, as sure of operation as the law of gravity. To ignore it is to mark ourselves as ignorant, or indifferent, either of which will destroy our chances of success.

6. Salesmanship

No matter how competent we may be, unless we can sell our ideas to others we may fall short of success. Whether it is persuading the boss to implement a suggestion we have made, our colleagues to cooperate on a project, our subordinates to put out more effort, our ability to "sell" is essential to our success. If we sincerely believe in what we are selling, it is not difficult to project that to others.

Study the techniques of the best salespeople with whom you have had dealings. It may be the man who sold you your new car, the woman who closed the sale of your house, or the sales rep who sold your company a computer system. No matter the product or service, note that they approached the sale in a systematic and well-conceived manner.

We may not be selling a tangible item, but if we want a new concept to be adopted, following the style of those successful salespeople will enhance our chances for success.

In Chapter 4 of this book, in which we discuss how to suggest and initiate change, specific guidelines and approaches on how to sell our ideas are presented.

7. Stick-to-it-iveness

One of the chief reasons people fail is that they give up too easily. Successful people will persevere despite obstacles to achieve their goals. It was only after thousands of failures that Edison developed the filament that made his first electric bulb work. It is easy to be discouraged when hard work does not bear fruition.

It is so tempting to give up. Keep in mind that old adage: "If at first you don't succeed, try again and again." New approaches or fresh viewpoints may be all that is needed.

> *Most people give up just when they're about to achieve success. They quit on the one-yard line. They give up at the last minute of the game, one foot from a winning touchdown.*
>
> Ross Perot

Determination is the armor against which the missiles of adversity rattle harmlessly. We must instill in our minds the fact that when we give will the reins and say drive, we are headed toward the heights.

Hardly a single great invention has been placed on the market without a number of people putting forth the claim that they had the idea first—and in many cases they proved the fact. But when problems arose which stalled their progress, they gave up, while the person who refused to surrender and kept at it, overcame the problems and made the invention viable. Think of Mark Zuckerberg and the Winklevoss brothers.

The most wonderful idea is quite valueless until the inventor makes it work and puts it into practical operation. The government rewards the person who first gets a patent or first puts his or her invention into practical use—and the world does likewise. Thus, the dreamer must always lag behind the doer.

Every person willing to pay the price can be successful. The price is not in money, but in effort. The first essential quality for success is the desire to do something—to be something. The next thing is to learn how to do it. The next is to carry it to execution. It follows that the person best able to accomplish anything is the one with a broad mind—the one that has acquired knowledge. So, to be successful, we must be free-thinking, must acquire all the knowledge that we can and stick to our task until it is completed to our satisfaction.

Another aspect of stick-to-itive-ness is to always try to improve ourselves, no matter where we are or what our position is. Learn all that you can. Don't see how little you can do, but how much you can do. You will always be in demand, for you'll establish the reputation of being a hustler. There is always room for a hustler. Progressive firms never let a hustler leave their employment if they can help it.

Those that reach the top are the gritty, purposeful, hard workers and never the timid, uncertain, slow workers. Inexperienced people are seldom put in a position of responsibility and power. The individuals selected are those that have done something, achieved results in some project, or have taken the lead in their department. They are placed there because of their reputation of putting energy into their efforts, and also because they have previously shown that they have backbone and determination.

Those that are chosen at a crucial time are not usually geniuses. They do not possess any more talent than others, but they have learned that results can only be produced by untiring, concentrated effort. They know that miracles do not just happen. The only way they happen is if on sticks to a proposition and sees it through. That is the only secret of why some succeed and others fail. Successful people get used to seeing things accomplished and always feel sure of success. People that are failures get used to seeing failure. They expect it and attract it to themselves.

Sum and Substance

With the right kind of training every person can be successful. It is really a shame that so many men and women, rich in ability and talent, are allowed to go to waste. They have lost their grip on themselves. Somewhere along the line, through some indisposition, these people weakened their will, or through some sorrow or misfortune, became discouraged. At first all they need is a little help to get them back on their feet, but usually they get a knock and they go down instead. The result is that their latent powers never develop, and both they and the world are the losers. These people can be saved. All they need to be shown is that they have within them the power to change. Their minds only have to be turned from despair to hope in order to make them regain their hold.

When people lose their grip today, they must win redemption by their own will. They will get little encouragement or advice of an inspiring nature. Today we must conquer our weakening tendencies alone. We cannot depend on anyone to help. It is up to us to take one big brace, make firm resolutions, and resolve to conquer our weaknesses and vices. No one can do this for us. They can encourage us, that is all.

There is nothing that should interfere with our becoming successful. There is no handicap, not even poor health, which cannot be overcome if we apply more determination and grit and willpower.

By applying the seven "S" factors, our chances for success in all of your endeavors will be greatly enhanced. In addition to the qualities discussed above, here are eleven suggestions to guide you on your journey to achievement in your jobs and in your lives:

1. Success means successful living. When we are peaceful, happy, joyous, and doing what we love then, we are successful.
2. Find out what you love to do, and then do it. If you don't know your true expression, ask for guidance, and the idea will come.
3. Specialize in a particular field and try to know more about it than anyone else.
4. A successful person is not selfish. His or her main desire in life is to serve humanity.
5. There is no true success without peace of mind.
6. A successful person possesses great psychological and spiritual understanding.
7. If we imagine an objective clearly, we will be provided with the means to achieve it through the wonder-working power of our mind.
8. Our thought, fused with feeling, becomes a subjective belief, and according to our belief is it done unto us.
9. The power of sustained imagination draws forth the miracle-working powers of our mind.
10. If you are seeking promotion in your work, imagine your employer, supervisor, or loved one congratulating you on your promotion. Make the picture vivid and real. Hear the voice, see the gestures, and feel the reality of it all. Continue to do this often, and through frequent visualization, you will experience the joy of the answered prayer.
11. The idea of success contains all the elements of success. Repeat the word "success" to yourself frequently with faith and conviction, and you will be under a subconscious compulsion to succeed.

2

THE IMPORTANCE OF MAKING CHANGES

Change is the law of life. And those who look only to the past or present are certain to miss the future.

John F Kennedy

There's no doubt that the world is changing at a rate never before experienced or even imagined. Whole industries are born and extinguished—seemingly overnight. The businesses that lead, anticipate, and benefit from these rapid changes have in many cases become tremendously successful. Those that were unprepared, surprised or overwhelmed, however, found themselves falling behind their competitors. Many of these organizations have sustained major losses or have completely gone out of business.

One way in which companies fail to meet the challenge of change is complacency with the long-established systems and procedures in which they have always worked. They've become slaves to the culture—the organizational way of life—in which they are comfortable.

If we are to survive, we must look at the thought processes that our organizations follow with a sense of constructive discontent. We must determine whether the practices that we are using are bringing the desired results or not. If they're not, we must be prepared to make whatever changes are needed to guide the organization to improvement and success.

It was not so long ago that it was rare to see a computer on the desk of an executive. Computer use was limited to specialists who would provide printouts to managers for their use. Today, the computer is an essential tool and can be found on the desks of every executive. Instead of depending on reports from specialists, real-time information is at his or her fingertips. Computerized design and drafting, computer-aided manufacturing, robotics and continually changing technologies have become part of the most progressive organizations.

These changes have compelled organizations to reexamine and restructure those aspects of their cultures that involve technology.

There is nothing permanent except change.

Heraclitus

However, change is not limited to technological matters. Many successful managers make a practice of periodically evaluating every process, practice, and system used in their company. Whether we are in management or are associates who are involved in the process, we should commit ourselves to keep seeking improvements in the way our jobs are done and be supportive of changes that will accomplish them.

In addition, due to the restructuring of many organizations leading, in many cases, to downsizing and outsourcing, so employee morale has often fallen to new depths. The unconditional loyalty and dedication of employees, who looked upon their jobs as careers and their employment as relatively secure, have been replaced in a good number of these companies resulting in uncertainty and skepticism. A new organizational culture must be developed to overcome these concerns and renew in the staff an attitude of commitment and cooperation.

Indeed, over the past several years new concepts of personnel management have come into being that have increased productivity, enriched the workplace and stimulated creativity and innovation. It is much easier to obtain recognition and acceptance of technical change than it is for managers to change the way they deal with people.

Challenges of Change Engagement

Every time something significant changes in an organization, challenges arise as a result. Some of the challenges are personal, some evolve within work teams, and some challenges emerge across the organization. To successfully engage organizational change, we need to be aware of the challenges and be prepared to deal with them professionally and confidently.

Change typically generates at least some resistance. Individuals often feel that they are losing power, autonomy, or resources due to a changing work environment. As a result, they cling to the status quo. To assure success, we must challenge ourselves and persuade others to lower their resistance and focus on positive outcomes.

One of the biggest challenges of change engagement is simply getting people to take change seriously. During periods of change, individuals often take a "wait and see" attitude, neither embracing nor resisting the change. Our challenge is to inspire ourselves and the people with whom we work to embrace change, support it, and even become champions for it.

Minimizing Anxiety

> *We all have big changes in our lives that are more or less a second chance.*
>
> Harrison Ford

Most of us experience great anxiety when changes that will affect us are proposed. Individuals are more likely to embrace change, and teams function more successfully, when anxiety is at a minimum. Our action plan in minimizing anxiety is to understand the plan for change, to express our level of commitment to the plan, and to recognize that the plan and our role in it will evolve during the change.

Gaining Cooperation

Any change in our organization may create breakdowns in cooperation. During change, organizations often find that cooperation and communication among departments, teams, and even individual employees are at risk. As participants in the change, we are challenged to break down those walls and build bridges of cooperation between organizational functions.

When the work environment is changing, there is typically confusion over priorities. If we get a new manager, for instance, what will he or she think is the most important priority? If we are to come out of the change successfully, what should we focus on first? This challenge is met through careful and thorough communication. We cannot succeed by using a dictatorial, military model of management. We need every erg of energy and creativity our employees can contribute to remain competitive in today's fastmoving, highly competitive business world.

Determine How Staff Perceives the Situation

> *It had long since come to my attention that people of accomplishment rarely sat back and let things happen to them. They went out and happened to things.*
>
> Leonardo da Vinci

Before any action can be initiated, it is important to determine how the people involved perceive the situation. Dale Carnegie and Associates, Inc. has developed a system for this purpose. It is called the "Change Engagement Innerview." This can be conducted by the supervisor with his or her staff, by a consultant, or a member of management. Another approach is to have the staff members conduct these "innerviews" with each other. The purpose is twofold. The first is to deepen the understanding of how the staff members may react to change. The second is for the people being "innerviewed" to gain a deeper understanding of their own reaction to change. The "innerview" consists of three categories of questions.

Factual Questions

The first group of questions revolves around obtaining relevant information. For example, if the change involves changing the way a job will be performed:

- How will you perform this part of the job now?
- What aspects do you find easiest to do?
- What aspects are more difficult?
- If you could change an aspect of the job, what would you do?

Causative Questions

Causative questions determine the motives or causative factors behind some of the factual questions. These are typically "why" and "how" questions.

- How do the methods now in use help or hinder reaching the goals of the department?
- Why do they hinder or help?
- What do you particularly like about the current methods? Why?
- What do you particularly dislike about the current methods? Why?

Value-Based Questions

Lastly, value-based questions help us connect to the person's value systems and the worth they place on things.

- What is one workplace change that stands out in your memory?
- What was your initial reaction to that change?
- What was the final outcome of the change?
- What did you learn about yourself?
- What is the strength that you see in yourself?
- How did you see that strength impact you in that situation?
- Tell me about a time that this strength was used in another situation.

The Change Model

Engaging workplace change can be an unpredictable experience, because processes and people evolve in diverse ways as they undergo change. No two individuals will respond in exactly the same way to workplace changes. In the same way, identical changes implemented in multiple areas of an organization produce distinctly different outcomes.

The following Change Model shows how you can stay on top of the change engagement process by thoroughly preparing for it, while allowing for various outcomes. This model allows us to take a structured approach to organizational change and still maintain flexibility.

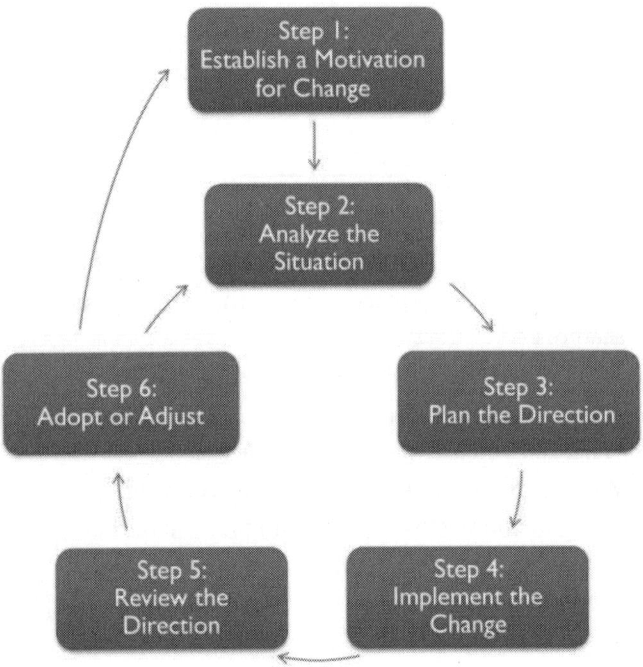

Step 1 Motivation for Change

The Change Model begins at the point where the organization finds a motivation for change. Sometimes external issues drive the change, like reorganizations, management overhauls, relocations, or acquisitions/mergers. Other times internal forces drive the change, such as upgraded technology, or expansions in product lines or services.

Step 2 Analyze the Situation

As the organization becomes progressively more motivated to change, leadership undertakes a thorough analysis of the risks and opportunities associated with the proposed change.

- What are the potential gains in undertaking the change?
- What are the costs?
- What are the risks of making the change?
- What are the risks of not making the change?

Step 3 Plan the Direction

Once the determination is made that opportunities outweigh the risks of making the change, a plan is developed for change implementation. Many organizational change initiatives fail because of lack of careful, thorough planning. In this step of the model, the stage is set for the ultimate success or failure of the change. Key elements of the plan must include:

- Planning for the impact of the change on individuals who will be most affected.
- Planning for the impact of the change on the systems within the organization that will be most affected.

- Developing a step-by-step plan for integrating the change into the organization.
- Establishing a review plan to measure the success of the proposed change.

Step 4 Implementing the Change

Depending on the type and scope of the change, implementation within the organization may be gradual or abrupt. Changes such as layoffs or acquisitions often are implemented with little prior warning, while staffing, reorganization, or technology changes may be phased in over a period of time. The management's most critical role in this step of the change process is to maintain open, honest lines of communication with each other and the staff.

- Define individual responsibilities. Although change usually affects many individuals, each person involved has a specific role. Bill may be responsible for phase A, Sue for phase B, etc. Clarifying what each person is expected to do in as much detail as necessary is the key to accomplishing the goal.
- Announce and launch the change. If the change is relatively minor, a meeting of the leader with his or her staff is usually enough to set the stage and get it started. In more complex changes, several meetings may have to be held at different levels. Everybody involved must understand what is to be done not only by that person and that team, but what each of the other participating units will be doing and how they will interface.
- Adhere to timetables. Timetables for each phase of the project should be clear to everyone and steps to catch

deviations should be made so that no one phase falls behind, holding up the entire project.

- Restate the benefits. At the start of the change process, all participants should be sold on the benefits to them of the change. Periodically during the change process, these benefits should be reiterated to all involved as a means of reinforcing their motivation.

Step 5 Review the Direction

Once the change has been implemented, we monitor the outcomes of the new structure and system. As team members in a changing work environment, one can't assume that the change will evolve exactly as planned, or that every individual affected by the change will react as anticipated. Your role is to set and regularly review checkpoints that will reveal whether the change is working as anticipated and is producing the desired results.

- Establish ways of measuring results. Ways of measuring results may be quantitative or qualitative, or where neither method is not feasible, by setting specially designed criteria.
- Communicate criteria for successful change outcomes. It is best for the criteria to be written in a manual, work orders or memoranda—and reinforced by training meetings and person-to-person discussions with each person involved. Coordinate the gathering and measuring of change effects. Not only members of our work group or team, but all others who are affected should be aware of the criteria and follow-up.
- Inform key team members consistently during the

review process. Let team members know if and when deviations occur and work with them to correct them.

Step 6 Adopt or Adjust

- If the review process concludes that the change is not working as planned, adjustments need to be made to the change implementation. Assuming that your change analysis and plan have been executed accurately, you ought to be able to adjust the implementation of the change in order to achieve your desired results. Here is a guide to accomplishing this:
- Determine where the outcomes are falling short of your plan.
- Engage key individuals in determining adjustments that need to be made.
- Keep the lines of communication open with everyone involved.
- Make adjustments to the review process as well as the change implementation.

Four Fundamental Plan Precepts

Plans that have been most successful follow four fundamental precepts:

1. They are simple. Written in clear, uncomplicated language, plans that succeed are easily understood by the people who are responsible for making them work. Instead of theories and rationales, they provide common-sense approaches to dealing with the situations that arise.

2. They do not curtail creativity. Each goal is carefully phrased to avoid misinterpretation. However, the basic plan does not include details. Strategies and tactics are left open to be developed as the plan moves along. This does not tie down the implementing group. It enables the group's members to react with flexibility and encourages them to use their own creativity in fleshing out the plan.
3. They concentrate on immediate results. Although, the long-term objectives are never out of mind, in order to build momentum and establish credibility, people want to see immediate results. By accomplishing specific changes early in the process, it encourages everybody to move upward and onward.
4. They stress on the benefits of the change. Unlike the traditional approach to planning which concentrates on the "what," "where," and "how," an effective plan for change emphasizes the "why." When people understand why what is planned will benefit the company and themselves, it reinforces their commitment.

Most of the change we think we see in life is due to truths being in and out of favor.

Robert Frost

Taking a Creative Approach to Change

Engaging change professionally means engaging your creativity. Since your environment will essentially be new after the change, what better time to be innovative and creative? By thinking and acting creatively, you can make the change process more exciting and more of a professional growth experience, and you can achieve more dynamic and interesting outcomes. To tap into your creative potential, remember these guidelines:

- *Keep an open mind.*
  Too often we impede the creative process by looking at what won't work, rather than what will. We stifle creativity with closed minds and too much focus on barriers. Even if an idea seems out of place at first, keep an open mind, allow the idea to grow and see what becomes of it.
- *Study.*
  We don't have to create solutions out of thin air. Many organizations have experienced change. Scores of books have been written on the subject. Study how others have successfully negotiated changing work environments and build on their ideas.
- *Dialogue.*
  Studies on organizational change have shown that individuals feel isolated during change, even if everyone else in the organization is experiencing the same changes. Talk to other individuals who have experienced similar changes. Dialogue with key people in the organization's change process to understand plans, goals, and the projected outcomes of the change in your organization.
- *Reflect.*
  Periods of change in the workplace are good opportunities to take a personal inventory. Ask yourself how can I expand my skills and knowledge by

fully participating in the change? How could I create new opportunities for myself? Where do I need to be more open and receptive to change?

- *Imagine.*

  Maybe this change is the opportunity of a lifetime for us. Why not imagine ways that we can make the best of this change, capitalize on it and reach new levels of skill and knowledge?

There is no limit to what you can imagine in terms of your career, as a result of creatively embracing change in the workplace.

Energizing Ourselves for Change

One of the challenging results of change is that it can leave us feeling fatigued. All of your efforts are focused on new tasks, responsibilities and relationships. Because of this, you need to look for ways to maintain, and even increase our personal energy during times of change. Some strategies for energizing ourselves include:

- *Create a vision.*

  Nothing is more personally motivating than creating a compelling vision. You must visualize yourself succeeding as a result of the change. Imagine the benefits of growing as a result of the change—creating new opportunities, and building a more exciting and dynamic future.

- *List opportunities.*

  What are the opportunities presented by the change? Make a list of all the ways that you can grow, add new skills, meet influential people, and add valuable experience to our resumes.

- *Create energy.*

  It's difficult to create energy in a vacuum. Most of us need the stimulation of other individuals and their ideas, input, feedback and support. Times of change offer an opportunity to add to your network of people who understand you, believe in you, and are willing to help you move forward.

- *Build bridges.*

  Changes in any organization normally involve the establishment of new relationships. Sometimes we resist these new relationships, especially, if it involves a new supervisor or perceived loss of our authority. Instead of retreating from the new relationships, you should draw energy from them by embracing them and building bridges between the people you encounter and yourself. Meeting new people is usually highly energizing, because you find commonalities in your values and goals, and the creativity of collaboration.

Reinforce Motivation

When faced with change, many people need to reinforce their motivation. Here are twelve suggestions to help accomplish this:

1. Have patience. What seems like an eternity now will seem like a "flash" in the years ahead.
2. Take just one day at a time and trust that you'll have everything you truly need.

3. Be willing to face what is happening. Test out the new realities with a friend who knows and can support you.
4. Practice letting go of the old, so the new can emerge.
5. Spend time learning about the change.
6. Look for the opportunity. "What's in it for me?" is not always obvious. Keep looking.
7. Stay in charge of your attitude. You can make the day as bright as you choose.
8. Let go of the need to control. When you do, breakthrough happens.
9. Prepare yourself for something new. No door is ever closed without another one being opened.
10. Feel your fears and do the scary things anyway. Think of fear as energy in disguise.
11. Trust the process. The path will open. The answers will come.
12. If it is up to you to make the change work. Take personal ownership.

The Most Common Mistakes When Making Changes

There are eight common mistakes made when managing change in organizations. These mistakes undermine the good intentions of the change and they foster resistance and lack of individual commitment. By avoiding these mistakes, one can be more successful in getting everyone in the organization to embrace the recommended changes.

1. *Implementing too much change in too short a time frame.*

   Individuals can handle only so much change at one time

without feeling overwhelmed and burned out. In managing change, look carefully at the timing of new initiatives. Ask which changes are most urgent and need to be addressed today and which changes can be introduced later. Not only will people be more cooperative, they will be more productive before, during and after the changes have been implemented.

2. *Lack of a long-term change vision and strategy.*

   Too often in organizations, the decision is made to implement the changes now and deal with the outcomes later. For change to be managed professionally, a clear long-term vision needs to be developed and communicated within the organization, and a strategy needs to be designed that goes far beyond the initial implementation stage of the change.

3. *Not making a convincing case for change.*

   Just because the management of the organization understands the need for change doesn't mean the rest of the organization's staff sees the purpose. People need to be convinced that the change has value and is worth embracing. We achieve this by making and communicating a solid case for change, supported by relevant evidence.

4. *Limited individual skills.*

   Some changes such as promotions and transfers, tend to push individuals to the limits of their business skills. You need avoid this mistake by preparing and training individuals ahead of time, when possible, or immediately upon implementing the change.

5. *Shortage of organizational resources.*

   Many change initiatives that start promisingly end up withering and dying from lack of necessary resources. Part of the role of managing change is to ensure that the organization is committing the necessary resources of time, money and manpower to see the change successfully through to completion.

6. *Leadership resistance to changing roles.*

   When the leadership of the organization resists change, the success of the initiative is severely jeopardized. Typically, that resistance occurs when leaders see an eroding of their control or responsibility as an outcome of the change. Leaders need the most flexibility of anyone in the organization in order for the change to succeed.

7. *Failing to integrate and align all change initiatives.*

   Every process that changes within an organization impacts the processes that are integrated and aligned with it. For example, a software change not only affects everyone who uses it, but also every other software program that interfaces with it and every customer, vendor or employee who is in the network of that software.

8. *Poor follow-through, measurement, and monitoring of change outcomes.*

   How well was the change accepted and embraced? How much were systems and processes improved by the change? What additional changes could make the initiative even more successful? These kinds of questions are too often never asked, and as a result, there is little sense of accomplishment or commitment to further change.

Managing Individuals During Periods of Change

In his classic book, *How to Win Friends and Influence People*, Dale Carnegie presented a time-proven set of guidelines on winning people over to one's ideas. Here are a few of these tenets that are particularly applicable in dealing with people in the change-making process. (A complete list of these principles will be found in Appendix B of this book.)

- Begin with praise and honest appreciation.
- Call attention to the other person's mistakes indirectly.
- Talk about your own mistakes before criticizing the other person.
- Ask questions instead of giving direct orders.
- Let the other person save face.
- Praise the slightest improvement. Praise every improvement.
- Be hearty in your approbation and lavish in your praise.
- Give the other person a fine reputation to live up to.
- Make the fault seem easy to correct.
- Make the other person happy about doing the thing you suggest.

Managing Ourselves During Organizational Change

> *They always say time changes things, but you actually have to change them yourself.*
>
> Andy Warhol

If we are leaders, we are expected to model appropriate responses to change. Others in the organization look up to us to see how we react to workplace change. Because of this, we have to remember to stay in control of our actions and attitudes.

1. Avoid negative self-talk. Rephrase your thoughts of resentment or fear into thoughts of growth and opportunity.
2. Be open about your concerns. Allow others to understand your frame of mind.
3. Be realistic about the challenges of successfully coping with the change.
4. Gather information through questions and research. Be as informed about the change as possible. Use the "innerview" approach described earlier in this chapter.
5. Be as productive as you can in your current role. Focus on organizational and recordkeeping tasks, so that you are prepared to hand off current responsibilities to someone else. Be ready to demonstrate your competence.

Many of us are not leading the change, but are participants in the change. How we can accept and work with changes in which we are involved (but do not lead), will be discussed in Chapter 4.

Overcoming Fear

> *A competitive world has two possibilities. You can lose or if you want to win, you can change.*
>
> Lester C Thurow

Whether we lead or just participate in the process, most of us experience fear to some extent in a changing work environment. We don't know whether the change will impact us positively or negatively. We don't know how our future figures into the organization's change-management plan. We don't know whether the work we've been doing will be valued going forward. To succeed during times of change, we have to find ways of working through our fears.

Many people are afraid to try new ideas, new ventures, or unusual approaches to solving problems because they are afraid to fail. Fear of failure is a human trait. Nobody wants to suffer the pains of defeat, but no endeavor can succeed unless it is attempted and with every attempt there is the risk that it will not work.

All of us have failed in some of the things we try throughout our lives, but we learn from our mistakes and use what we learn to overcome them. The first time we try something new, it is likely we will not succeed.

Don't Give Up

Even when you have experience and know-how, you cannot always be successful. There will be times when you do fail, but you must not let the worry over failure overwhelm you. We learn from our mistakes and apply what we learn to our next ventures. R H Macy had to close his first seven stores, but instead of giving up as a "failure," he kept trying and became one of Americas leading retailers. Babe Ruth struck out over 1,300 times in his career, but that is forgotten because of his 714 home runs.

Seek the Cause

Thomas Edison never gave up in his quest to harness electricity, but perseverance alone was not enough. Each time one of his experiments failed, he studied what caused the failure and kept seeking solutions. It is said that he failed almost one thousand times before developing the filament that made the light bulb work.

Minimize Risk

All new ideas are risky. If an idea has not been proven successful in the past, there is a good chance that it may not succeed now.

When Paula developed a unique marketing plan for the introduction of a new product her company had developed, she recognized that there were many unknowns that might defeat her objective. To identify what roadblocks might be encountered, she chose to test-market the product in three cities before developing the final plans for national distribution. From each test, she was able to learn probable problem areas and work to overcome them. By the time the national marketing campaign started, most of the bugs had been detected and corrected and the chances of success greatly increased.

Seek Alternative Solutions

If the program Paula developed did not work and work quickly, the company would be in serious difficulties. She knew that her idea was good, but it was new and had never been tried. If it failed, there would be no time to evaluate the reasons and make adjustments. It just had to work immediately. To protect herself and the company in the event that there were problems with the new program, Paula developed an alternative solution, less innovative and unlikely to be as effective as the basic plan, but that would at least serve as an interim solution. If the basic plan did not succeed, the problem would at least be under control. Further study could then be made to determine why the plan had not worked and additional steps taken to enable it to succeed.

Psych Ourselves to Succeed

When any plan or concept fails, the persons involved with it are likely to be depressed and some may easily give up. We must expect that failures occur and from time to time we may face defeat.

Andrea was devastated. She was so sure that her suggestions would have solved a problem her department had encountered, but despite all of her efforts, they just didn't do the job. "I'm a failure," she thought. "I'm just not up to this kind of challenge." If this attitude persisted, not only would Andrea remain unhappy, but it would also prevent her from thinking clearly about additional ways to tackle the problem.

Accept that all of us fail from time to time, and that it is not anything to be ashamed of. You should give ourselves a pep talk, and remind yourself that failures are part of trying new things. Unless you continue to innovate, you will be become stagnant. Remember all of the successes you have had—often after previous failures—and keep telling yourself that you've done it before and you can do it again. Failure is a temporary situation. You can and will overcome it and succeed again.

Obtain Full Commitment of All Participants

In order for any change to not just be accepted by the affected people but fully endorsed, all staff members must be fully committed to its success. Managers who lead successful change efforts stimulate their personnel and inspire them to commit wholeheartedly to the project. Here are ten precepts that outstanding managers apply to obtain and maintain the commitment of their associates:

1. They only make promises they know they can keep. Claude, the vice president of international business for a computer software company elaborated on this idea. "As a senior executive I am often tempted to make promises to people based on what I am almost sure will occur. But, I know that if something develops which may make it impossible to fulfill that promise, even though it was made in good faith, it will reflect on my integrity. I make damn few promises and keep them all."
2. They avoid exaggeration or overstatement. A public relations executive reported that in order to promote her clients' organizations, it was very tempting to overstate information or stretch the truth—just a little. But, she attested, "Knowledgeable people will not be fooled and in the long run it will hurt the client."
3. Outstanding managers set realistic goals—and then exceed expectations. It always looks better to give more than is expected. Some managers set low goals so that is easy to exceed them. This can be self-defeating because if goals are too low, not only will the results be mediocre, but also the people working on the project will be unchallenged. Reasonable goals that can be attained with hard work stimulate people to commitment—and exceeding the goals makes their attainment that much sweeter.
4. They tell the truth—even when it hurts. A renowned example of this occurred in 1982. McNeil Laboratories, manufacturers of Tylenol, had discovered that several bottles

of their product had been contaminated with cyanide. The CEO immediately announced that the company was recalling the entire inventory and replacing it with new tamper-proof packages. This cost the company millions of dollars, but its forthright acknowledgment and action reinforced the reputation for integrity of McNeil and its parent company, Johnson and Johnson.

5. They practice what they preach. Many organizations put great emphasis on improving the quality of their products. Their executives give speeches about the importance of empowering the employees to make decisions, yet in their own companies, there is only lip service to this concept. Jack Welch, long-time CEO of General Electric Company practiced what he preached. He set up a program to assure that all GE employees would be fully committed to GE's quality improvement mission.

   Welch implemented an innovative management technique called "Work-Out," which encouraged open communication and the sharing of ideas. Work-Out is essentially a forum where workers and management meet regularly to determine "What's the matter with this place and how can we make it better?" Work-Out peels away layers of management and empowers workers to share ideas and reduce the amount of time it takes to get a quality product from the plant to the customer.

   At GE's Lynn, Massachusetts plant, Charles Reuter, a union leader pointed out how the program had changed the attitude of the union and its members toward the company. He said: "People are listening, and the areas we disagree in are becoming smaller. Work-Out caused a culture shock in some of the old-line middle management, who used to say, "You're a grunt and I'm the boss so shut up and do it my way."

6. Exceptional managers admit their mistakes—quickly. As the old adage says, "To err is human." We all make mistakes. Failure to acknowledge that one is wrong only compounds the situation.

   Effective managers don't make excuses or try to rationalize decisions that didn't work out as planned. They investigate the reasons for the problem, and work to make the necessary corrections and adjustments to bring the program back on track.

   When Coca Cola changed its formula to the "New Coke" in the mid-eighties, it made the change after months of market studies and experimentation. Despite the tremendous amount of work and money spent in planning the revamped product, the public did not like the New Coke and sales plummeted.

   Management could have rationalized that the market studies were right and all that was needed was time to get the customers used to the new taste. They could have attempted to justify their decision by pointing out the statistics, analysis, and "scientific" studies that had been made. But they didn't. Roberto Goizueta, Coke's CEO at that time, immediately reintroduced the old standard product, re-christened it "Classic Coke," and turned what could have been a major catastrophe into a marketing coup.

If you're not making mistakes, then you're not doing anything. I'm positive that a doer makes mistakes.

John Wooden

7. They do their homework. Instead of relying on hunches or superficial information, successful managers get all the facts straight before making decisions. They are not reluctant to ask for help from others, including subordinates, to obtain ideas and suggestions. They investigate what other organizations have done when they faced similar problems and make necessary adaptations.
8. Outstanding managers are superb communicators. They encourage enthusiasm for the concepts they present, whether directed to their own people or to outsiders. They encourage others to bring out and develop their own ideas. Their enthusiasm is contagious.
9. They relate to people at a human level. Organizational changes start with the people in the organization. Managers must understand the psychology of the people with whom they are dealing. People differ and what is important to one may not be important to another.
10. They always follow-up and follow-through. Richard is an example of a man who didn't follow-up. When he was appointed vice president of operations of his company, he gave the three department managers who reported to him a great deal of autonomy. "They are trained and competent managers," he thought. "Together we developed goals and objectives, and I can depend on them to fulfill their assignments."

    Richard concentrated his efforts on planning future programs and left the day-to-day operations to his managers. He assumed that they would carry out what had been agreed to. It didn't quite work out that way. By failing to follow-up to determine if the work was on target, errors were made and the decisions that were taken delayed timely completion of the assignments.

When you're finished changing, you're finished.

Benjamin Franklin

Sum and Substance

- To survive in this dynamic environment, you must look at the thought processes that your organizations follow with a sense of constructive discontent. If the practices that you are using are not bringing the desired results, you must be prepared to make whatever changes are needed to guide the organization to improvement and success.
- Individuals often feel that they are losing power, autonomy, or resources due to a changing work environment. To assure success, we must challenge ourselves and persuade others to lower their resistance and focus on positive outcomes.
- By using the "innerview" technique, we learn how the staff members may react to change and help the people being "innerviewed" to gain a deeper understanding of their own reaction to change.
- In making changes, follow the six-step change model:
    1. Establish a motivation for change
    2. Analyze the situation
    3. Plan the direction
    4. Implement the change
    5. Review the direction
    6. Adopt or adjust
- By thinking and acting creatively, we can make the change

process more exciting and more of a professional growth experience. And we can also achieve more dynamic and interesting outcomes.

- To assure success, review the 12 steps to making successful changes and the 8 common mistakes outlined in this chapter.
- Maintain your self-confidence during the change process. You will meet snags and defeats, but never give up.
- In order for any change to not just be accepted by the affected people but fully endorsed, all staff members must be fully committed to its success. Managers who lead successful change efforts stimulate their personnel and inspire them to commit wholeheartedly to the project.

3

ADJUSTING TO CHANGE

Everyone thinks of changing the world, but no one thinks of changing themselves.

Leo Tolstoy

Considering the ever-accelerating rate of change in today's workplace, there may be no more important skill than to adjust successfully to change. Sometimes, adjusting to change comes easily. We enjoy the challenge and opportunity that the change presents. Other times, we find ourselves resisting change, focusing on what we might lose as a result of the change, rather than on what we might gain. Our ability to adjust to workplace change is usually observed by leaders and team members, so it is important to adapt productively and positively, no matter how we might feel personally about the change.

In this chapter, we will discuss the different aspects of workplace change that we may have to face. It is essential that we examine ways of adapting our attitudes and to commit to adapting our work patterns to more successfully meet the challenges of change. We must examine ways of adapting our attitudes so that we are ready to meet the difficulties of a changing work environment. We must be flexible and productive when change happens, so that we make a positive impression on others in the organization.

The Challenge of Change

The office was in chaos. Everybody was buzzing around. A notice on the bulletin board announced a meeting of all department heads at 10 AM. What was going on? One thing was sure. Something important was in the works.

At 10 AM, they assembled in the conference room. The CEO called the meeting to order and announced: "We are going to make a major change in our order-processing system that affects every department in the organization." He then went on to specify details.

After the meeting, all of us were pretty shaken up. Most of us were happy with the current system. We knew it well and had worked on it for years. We were comfortable doing our jobs and now it would all change. Some of us were fearful that our jobs might be eliminated under the new system or that our department might be absorbed by another department and we would be demoted.

> *Progress is impossible without change, and those who cannot change their minds cannot change anything.*
>
> George Bernard Shaw

What steps can management take to overcome these concerns and assure that the change will not only be accepted but also enthusiastically implemented?

Change is not always welcome and is often resisted. Why? When people perform a task in a specific way for a time, they are comfortable doing it that way only. Change takes them out of their comfort zone—and that's a problem for most people. But in order to make progress, change is not only necessary, it is important (and inevitable) for successful operations.

There are specific challenges that occur when we initiate organizational change. In order to meet these challenges, we need to be creative, energetic and flexible. In this chapter, we will analyze those challenges of change engagement and the ways they impact us personally and professionally. We will learn a model for organizational change, and determine our role in moving the organization through this change model successfully.

Individually, we have a variety of reactions to change, depending on how we perceive it affecting our organization and ourselves. We face the challenge of adapting to change in the organization by adapting our attitudes, and emotions.

> *Action and reaction, ebb and flow, trial and error, change—this is the rhythm of living. Out of our over-confidence, fear; out of our fear, clearer vision, fresh hope. And out of hope, progress."*
>
> Bruce Barton

Moving Out of Our Comfort Zone

Changing our responsibilities provokes anxiety and leaves us feeling outside of our comfort zone. As a professional, we can expect to be pushed to the edges of our comfort zones again and again as we add to our experience and responsibility, and as we try to adapt to workplace change.

Flexibility

Your organization may have expectations of you during change. This may require letting go of your old way of thinking about your jobs. The role you play moving forward may be quite different from what you thought it would be. For change to succeed across the organization, everyone needs to be as flexible as possible. This can be a big challenge for you sometimes, especially if you feel that you are being pushed in a direction that you don't want to go in, or are even taking a step backward in your career.

Attitude Control

Your attitudes take a beating during times of change. Not only do you feel uncertain and uncomfortable, you sometimes have real issues with the change and don't feel positive about it at all. One day you might deal with it well. On another day, your fears and resentments overwhelm your positive thoughts, and you lose control of your attitude. When this happens, you contribute little or nothing to the change process.

In order to adjust to change, you need to confront those attitudes that slow you down, and replace them with attitudes that embrace the change that is occurring. In order to adjust your attitude, you might ask yourself these four questions:

1. In what ways do I need to change in this changing work environment?

2. Why do I want to embrace this change?
3. How do I know that I can be successful in adjusting to this change?
4. How willing am I to do what is needed to make this change work?

If you don't like something, change it. If you can't change it, change your attitude. Don't complain.

Maya Angelou

Adjusting Our Patterns

Throughout our careers, our roles and responsibilities are continually changing. Leading teams, leading meetings, communicating our vision and mission, are all challenges we are likely to confront as our careers progress. As we mentioned earlier, the ability to be truly adaptable may be more important than any other skill in determining our consistent, long-term success. The following principles will help you to effectively adjust your patterns:

Adjust expectations

Maybe that promotion is not going to happen this year, after all. Maybe you are not going to be reporting to the same person, or maintaining exactly the same responsibilities. You must adjust your expectations without lowering them, if possible. You must focus on goals that are within your control.

When Sally was hired as a store manager by the "Fashions for Teens" retail chain, she set her goal to be a regional manager within three years. She is now in her fourth year on the job and is not even close to reaching her goal. Her work has been excellent and her performance reviews strong.

Her failure to meet her goal was beyond her control. The year she was hired, the company opened five stores and planned to continue this expansion. However, as the economy stalled, no new stores were opened and it might be years before the expansion is resumed. Sally has to adjust her expectations. Her choices include being patient and waiting for the economy to improve, examining what other opportunities are available in the company and seeking a regional management position in another chain.

> *The most powerful agent of growth and transformation is something much more basic than any technique: a change of heart.*
>
> John Welwood

When faced with disappointment on not getting the promotion or assignment desired, you should ask yourself these ten questions:

1. How can I make my current work more valuable to the company?
2. What can I do for this company that I am not now doing?
3. In what way can I improve how things are done in my department?
4. What new and different aspects of the work should I learn so that I can be more valuable to this organization?
5. What steps might I take to let my bosses know I am willing to accept more responsibility?
6. What can I learn about what other departments are doing that might fit into my goals?

7. If I have gone as far as I can in my current job, are there other jobs within the organization that I can do?
8. Are there assignments other people are reluctant to do that I might volunteer for?
9. How can I improve my accomplishments as a manager by getting my people to be better performers?
10. Am I willing to make the commitment and undergo the sacrifices and risks necessary to earn the right to move up the management ladder?

Build Relationships and Networks

Building your professional network is a fascinating and rewarding strategy for adapting to change. Assume that change is just around the corner. Who would you want to know or get to know better, if that change were to occur? Start to develop those relationships now and build a larger network of support and encouragement.

Computers fascinated Tim, a database operator at Lincoln Finance Company, just at the time his company was converting to an international computer network. He took advanced computer courses in the evening at a community college and hoped when the new systems were installed, he would be considered for transfer to the IT department. But when that time came, his request for transfer was rejected and the company hired someone else. Tim complained to his supervisor, who gave him this advice. "Tim, the company went outside because nobody in management knew about your computer skills. They only think of you as a database clerk. Get to know the new computer people, spend time with them and learn what they are doing and how they are functioning."

Over the next few months, Tim became friends with the computer staff and not only learned a lot, but also became known and was liked by them. When a new job opened in the department, they arranged for Tim's transfer.

Ask for Input

Another way to enhance your workplace network is to be aware that others in your organization may have insight into the ways that you can better adjust to change. You should make a practice of asking for ideas and suggestions and for feedback on how well you are adjusting to change. Periods of change are times to build bridges, not walls. They are times to be open to input, not defensive.

Practice Patience

When it comes to change, we often want to get it over with and move on as quickly as possible. The cycle of change in the workplace often takes longer than we expect. The change has to be communicated and integrated and there needs to be time for adjustment of all adjacent organizational functions. Individuals too, need time to adjust to changing work environments. What is the sense of tearing down old walls, to just build new ones? Your job is to challenge yourself to try at least one new way of adjusting to change every day. Make it a positive and productive effort.

When we are faced with change, it is easy to think that we don't want it, or need it; that we can't do it, or that we simply won't do it. Every day we see examples in the workplace of people exhibiting these attitudes. They are common during times of change. These attitudes are unproductive and unlikely to lead to much success or recognition on our part.

Develop an Attitude of Constructive Discontent

Many managers find it difficult to adjust to change. There are people in positions of leadership, although not despots or tyrants, who may resent disagreement and subtly repress ideas that differ from theirs. Although, they don't manage by fear, but they do not encourage opposing views. Such managers have to be sold on the importance of listening to other opinions and being openminded.

For example, organizations sincerely desirous of changing from an authoritarian to a more participative culture make a conscious effort to invite dissent, dissatisfaction and disagreement. They view it as part of a process of continuous improvement. They recognize that it leads to breakthroughs in thinking and can be enormously effective. They believe it is essential to the long-term interests of the business.

Psychologists call this approach to organizational interaction *constructive discontent*. One of the basic elements of culture change is to foster this attitude throughout the organization. The following approaches have helped many organizations in developing and maintaining a climate of constructive discontent not only in management but also throughout the organization.

1. Let people know that disagreement is not a capital offense. Not only will one not be punished for dissenting; it will be viewed favorably by supervisors and company management.
2. Managers and supervisors should treat all viewpoints with respect. Even if in their opinion the idea is not valid, effective managers let the proposer know it will be seriously considered. And they do consider it. Their

initial reaction may be biased, based on inadequate information, or just plain wrong.

3. Never ridicule the opinions of others. Even if an idea appears to be trivial, poorly conceived, or downright ridiculous, treat it as an honest effort. When rejecting it, present the rejection in the same way that more serious suggestions are presented.
4. Hold no grudges. You often find that some people appear to always oppose your ideas. Don't consider this a personal matter. Remember that only through open disagreements can ideas be brought out and evaluated.

   For example, we may have a staff member—like Jason—who disagrees for the sake of disagreeing. Such people can be nuisances, but if they see that we are serious about listening to their ideas and are not riled by their continuous disagreements, they will often stop their trivial dissents. Jason got a kick out of irking the boss. When he realized that the manager was not annoyed by these dissents and indeed, encouraged disagreements, he channeled his thinking into more constructive avenues.
5. Don't let pride of authorship or ownership keep you from seeing other people's viewpoints. Many managers become defensive about protecting their own ideas. Just because you suggested the idea being discussed, you shouldn't resent disagreement. It is, especially, important that you keep an open mind. The goal is to do the best for the company—not to aggrandize yourself or anybody else.

6. Don't play favorites. It is tempting to accept ideas from favored people and reject those of others. People who may not appear to be as bright or as diligent as others in the group may still come up with winning concepts.
7. Put the emphasis on doing *what's* right—not *who's* right. In evaluating suggestions, the focus of your analysis should be on the *content* of the material not the *source*.
8. Train yourself and your staff to keep these two questions in mind concerning everything you do: Is what you are doing the very best way to deal with this situation? If not, in what ways can you improve it? Methods change, management concepts change, organizational goals change. These two questions should be asked periodically to assure that what you are doing is not only on the cutting edge of the current technology, but is also the result of objective thinking about the company's welfare.
9. Accept the fact that there are no stupid questions. Even questions that appear to be irrelevant often can identify problems that may not be obvious to you.
10. Listen. Develop the techniques of being an active and empathetic listener. By your actions and reactions when people discuss matters with you, you can turn them on or off. Staff members will want to talk to you because they know you truly listen.
11. Value the diversity in people and in their perspectives, opinions and perceptions. People from different cultures, different levels of education and different types of backgrounds bring with them varying viewpoints.

You can learn a lot from seeing things through their eyes.

12. Keep encouraging people to explore their opinions. Help staff members evaluate the merits and limitations of their ideas. Provide them with the tools they need to do this, such as access to data, research materials and books and articles in the areas involved.
13. Don't kill the messenger. Managers must know the truth and the truth is not always pleasant. Mistakes cannot be corrected or compensated for unless you know that they have been made—and know it as quickly as possible. In a culture where people are blamed for being the bearers of bad news, employees who perceive problems will be afraid to report them. Encourage people to be forthright in presenting information—good or bad.
14. Give recognition to staff members whose application of constructive discontent has resulted in positive changes. Consider tangible rewards where appropriate. Make a point of acknowledging their contributions at department meetings. Publish stories about the changes made and those who contributed to them in the company newsletter.
15. Establish a climate in the company or the department that stimulates cooperation, collaboration, and teamwork. Managers and team leaders at all levels should be trained to become participative leaders instead of dogmatic bosses. Training in good communications, creative thinking, and collaborative actions should be ongoing and reinforced in the day-to-day workings of the entire organization.

Personal Unhappiness with Successful Changes

Imagine that the changes instituted by the company are working out very well. Often these are changes that you have heartily endorsed, but now after some time, you realized we were happier with the old ways. This is not uncommon. The new methods may not be as much fun to engage in.

This type of discontent is not limited to lower-level staff members. It often occurs with senior executives, especially, founders of small businesses like Stanley, the founder and president of a growing software company. He built the business over the years to a multimillion dollar organization. Last year he hired a management consultant to streamline the operation and increase its efficiency. The result was even better than expected, but Stanley found that his own role was different from the past and although effective, not much fun. He was a creative person who loved developing products and under the new system was primarily involved with the operational aspects of the company. He sat down with the consultant to discuss this. Here are some of the suggestions the consultant made:

1. Take account of our business life. Stanley was now focusing mostly on the business aspects of the company, and neglecting the creative product development and marketing areas that he loved to do. It was this work that motivated him to start his own business in the first place. He was advised to delegate as much of the business end as possible to members of the staff who could handle it. This gave the staff a great opportunity to learn more about managing the business and gave Stanley more time to concentrate on the tasks he enjoyed and which had led to his success.

2. Connect with other business owners. Stanley was advised to make friends with other business owners. They have problems and concerns that are similar to his. Communicating with individuals who had experienced or were experiencing the same things he was, could provide invaluable insight into how to overcome these situations.
3. Set concrete, short-term goals. Maybe Stanley would benefit from some time spent accomplishing tasks in another aspect of his life. One of the key things one can do to re-focus is to set specific goals for each day, each week and each month. As each goal is reached, it prepares you for the next and it's also a great confidence-booster. If you are positive you are on the right track with your life, these actions will help you get there.

Note that we all have highs and lows in our careers, in which our energy can be at an all-time high or flagging. At times when we feel to be in a rut, it helps to remember to assess our current situations and set goals, thereby keeping ourselves motivated and moving forward.

Any change, even a change for the better, is always accompanied by drawbacks and discomforts.

Arnold Bennett

Surviving Downsizing

One of the most traumatic changes you may ever face on the job is the prospect of being laid off. You haven't been fired for poor performance or for violating some company rule. Business has fallen off and management is compelled to reduce their costs by "downsizing"—a euphemism for laying people off. Although, in some companies layoffs are based only on seniority, most organizations consider many other factors as well. Your chances of surviving can be significantly improved if you take steps to stand out as a valuable employee.

Be Good in What We Do

Unless we do our job well, all the plans we may make to survive a layoff will fall apart. Men and women who survive make every effort to learn all they can about their jobs, as well as the other functions of the department, and work to help the company meet its goals. Study the work that goes on in your company. Make suggestions as to how it can be improved. Above all, we should set high standards for ourselves and the people we supervise—and work to see that they are met.

Keep Up With Technology

In the dynamic world in which we live, things are always changing. This is obvious in technical and professional work, but all people, not just professional workers, must keep up with the state of the art in their fields. Diane, an office supervisor, subscribes to several magazines that deal with office administration. She always visits business equipment shows. As a result, she enabled her company to be among the first to take advantage of some of the new systems and equipment that became available, including a complete overhaul of their communications equipment. When her company consolidated several departments, eliminating some supervisory jobs, there was no question about keeping Diane.

Expand the Job

Kevin, one of several sales coordinators, was responsible for following through from the time a sale was made until the merchandise was shipped. If customers had problems with the product after they received the shipment, they had to deal with the Customer Service Department, which often had to get back to Kevin for the necessary information. Kevin developed a system to consolidate these functions. This resulted in much more work for him, but it increased his value to the company.

Act Positively

When Shirley heard that the company was planning to downsize, she became totally negative. She assumed that she would be laid off and this negative thinking reflected in her work and in her attitude. She slowed down, made more errors, criticized everything her supervisor suggested and essentially "quit" in anticipation of the layoff.

Her colleague, Vicki, was more positive. She thought: "I'm good, so I probably will be kept." She worked harder and more effectively. When special work was needed, she didn't hesitate to do it. She continued to contribute the same effort, energy and commitment to her job that she always had. There was little question in the mind of management which of these people to keep.

Be Flexible

Elliot had managed his store for two years and was proud to tell everybody that he was a manager. Unfortunately, due to economic conditions, the company found it necessary to close his store. Elliot was offered a position as assistant manager of another store. “How can I take a reduction in position?” Elliot thought. “How can I tell my friends I’m no longer a manager? Maybe I should look for a manager’s job with another chain.”

After careful thought Elliot realized that he was respected and appreciated by his company and that by being flexible, he could survive this temporary setback until he could resume the career path on which he had started before the unexpected change.

Although, taking the lower-level position in a different store in the chain involved less prestige and a lower income, it was better than having no job at all or moving to another company where he was an unknown person and had to start from scratch.

Prepare for a Move if Necessary

Because there are times when no matter what you do you cannot prevent loss of your job, you should be prepared to take steps to obtain a new job. You should always have an up-to-date resume. You can use the contacts you’ve developed in the present job to develop a network that can lead you to other jobs.

As mature adults we should be able to face both the good and bad in our careers. By contributing all that you can to your employer’s well-being, you can do your best to maximize your possibilities of surviving a downsizing. By careful planning and attention to the possibility of downsizing, you can prepare a new career elsewhere if that is necessary.

Sum and Substance

- We face the challenge of adapting to change in the organization by adapting our attitudes and emotions.
- The ability to be truly adaptive may be more important than any other skill in determining your consistent, long-term success.
- One of the basic elements of culture change is to foster an attitude of constructive discontent throughout the organization.
- By remembering to assess your current situations and to set goals, you can keep yourself motivated and keep moving forward!
- You haven't truly faced change head-on until you have faced the worst case scenario. Consider how the change might push you beyond your capabilities, might create negative consequences with managers and team members and how it might drain your energy and productiveness.
- Cooperate with the inevitable. You know that you can't avoid or deflect change. It's a part of everything you do in your careers. When you remind yourself of this you won't waste your time and your attitude fighting the inevitable.
- Be prepared for the unexpected. Your company may be forced to downsize. Take steps to minimize your chances of being laid off by maximizing your value to the organization.

4

SUGGESTING AND INITIATING CHANGE

In today's workplace, we are in a constantly evolving environment of change. Often, we encounter change in several areas of our career at the same time. When we hold management positions, we may be in the formal role of leading the change, but in many situations we are only participating in a wider change occurring in the organization.

Our aim is to be seen as leaders in driving change, even though we may not be the sponsor or leader in the change process. Gaining a reputation as a change advocate positively impacts the way you are viewed within the organization. It also has a significant constructive effect on the satisfaction and motivation you feel in your careers.

Let's examine the extent of your current interaction with changes that are being made. You must start by working on ways to stay flexible during change. In addition, you must develop a personal plan for advocating for and leading change in the organization, even though you may not be in a position of authority.

One of the key factors for spurring yourself to success is the strong commitment you must have for continuous improvement. No matter how effective methods, processes or ideas may be, the search for an even more proficient approach never ceases. You can no longer afford to be complacent. Such clichés as "If it ain't broken, don't fix it," no longer have a place in modern managerial thinking. You must replace that thinking with "If it still works, it's probably obsolete!" As we mentioned in the previous chapter, you should look at everything you do with constructive discontent.

Frank and Lillian Gilbreth, pioneers in "scientific management" encouraged us to keep seeking "the one best way," and once it was instituted, keep seeking still a better way. David McClelland, another pioneer in management thinking called this "achievement motivation." He based this on the concept that people have an innate desire to achieve and by developing this desire, workers will strive to excel.

Challenge Ourselves

Many men and women are dedicated to their jobs and get great satisfaction from the work they do. This attitude encourages them to keep working toward continuous improvement.

Commitment to continuous improvement is not limited to improvement of ourselves. If we are team leaders or supervisors, our own success is dependent upon the success of the people we supervise. We should institute programs—often very informal— that will stimulate them to keep seeking betterment in production, quality, and administration.

Stan Seifer, assistant to the president of Frequency Electronic Company, which employs six hundred people in the manufacture of hi-tech electronic devices, used no special program, but made a point of giving people a good name to live up to. Stan encouraged innovation and ideas, recognized good work on a regular basis, and instilled his staff members with pride in their work. This has paid off with hundreds of suggestions and ideas that have kept his company in the forefront of its industry.

Keep the Customer in Mind

The Lincoln Credit Union which provides banking services to its members, has added a new dimension to its search for continuing improvement. The staff surveys customers on a regular basis and has implemented suggestions from them that have resulted in several significant improvements in their service. This dedication to the customers' desire has also given the customers a sense of empowerment and has furthered loyalty to the business.

Whether your goal is fighting for the survival of your company in tough economic times, attempting to maintain its competitive position, or becoming the leader in your field, making changes that will lead to continuous improvement must permeate your thinking.

> *If there is anything that we wish to change, we should first examine it and see whether it is not something that could better be changed in ourselves.*
>
> Carl Jung

The Art of "Followership"

We are often frustrated when our boss does not take our suggestions seriously. One way to overcome this is to gain the respect of the boss by being a valuable staff member.

Be a Good Worker

The first ingredient of good "followership" is doing one's own job superbly. Professionalism is essential to success as a leader or a follower. Obviously, if you are good in what you do, the boss is going to be able to depend upon you, making his or her job that much easier and making you that much more valuable to the organization.

When Sandra started in her first job as a marketing assistant, she asked her father, a very successful executive, for some advice on being a good employee. He responded: "A good employee is an employee who keeps his boss's boss off his boss's back."

You have to make your boss look good. This begins by giving your best performance at all times, but that is just the start. By helping some of the less effective people in the department become more efficient, you not only help the department as a whole become more successful and make our boss look better, but you are displaying the characteristics that will make you stand out as potential leaders.

Anticipate the Boss's Needs

When Gloria returned to the office after visiting the Business Equipment Show at the Civic Center, she commented to her assistant, Steve, that she was particularly impressed by an electronic collator she had seen. Steve made it his first priority to get to the Civic Center and look at that collator. He picked up some literature and looked at some of the other collators that were exhibited. After he returned to the office, he researched manufacturers of related equipment online. He checked with companies that were using this type of collator to learn about how the equipment was working for them and compiled a file on the results of his investigation.

A few months later Gloria went over to Steve's office and said, "Steve, when I was at the Business Show, I saw a collator that seemed to have some potential for us, could you get me some information about it?" Steve reached into his desk and pulled out the file and handed it to her.

Sure, we may waste some time by researching matters that may never be pertinent, but when we work with somebody for any length of time, we get to know what is most likely to be of interest and our efforts will be on target most of the time. By anticipating the boss's needs, not only do you become more useful to that person, but you also develop the initiative and resourcefulness that will help you in your own career.

Help the Boss Clarify His or Her Thinking

Ivan had the reputation of being an iconoclast. He always seemed to disagree with company policies and was constantly bringing up ideas that were different from the company's procedures. He had been fired from two previous jobs because of this. When Ivan went to work for his current employer, he resolved to try to be less critical, but his nature overcame his resolution and before long he was again vociferously expounding his disagreements.

When his boss called him in for a private conference, Kevin expected to be terminated again. However, this boss took a different tack. "Kevin, you can drive people crazy, but you do something for me that nobody else has ever done. You make me rethink and reevaluate what I have often taken for granted. You provide a good service that is needed. Now, if you can learn to be more diplomatic, you could be a valuable employee."

Good leaders need followers who are not just sycophants; people who always agree with them. A good follower should not be afraid to call the boss's attention to flaws and potential problems in his or her proposals. In this way, the follower provides a service that will not only result in better management on the part of the leader, but also demonstrates that his or her original ideas and suggestions are worth thoughtful consideration.

The Seven Basic Elements of a Good Change Plan

In order for you to initiate a workable change in your company, you must get the approval of management. This may not always be easy to obtain, but if you present your suggestion with a well-designed plan, your chances of having it accepted are vastly enhanced. Here is a seven-step approach to creating a solid plan for a new idea.

1. Provide a clear, accurate sense of the "as-is" situation.

As pointed out earlier in this book, the first step in making any change is to have a clear picture of the current situation. Study the substantive information available including production figures, costs, time needed to complete tasks, etc. Augment this by using well-designed "innerviews" (see Chapter 2) so you can identify the real causes of problems and separate them from the symptoms. When we hide our heads in the sand and hope problems will go away, no change occurs. If the current system is holding the organization back, the factors that cause the problems must be uncovered and accepted. Only then can the steps be taken that will lead to a culture change.

2. Present a clear, reasonable vision of the "should be" situation.

Present to senior management and all persons involved in the change what the new system should look like. Goals should be developed that are attainable and acceptable to all.

3. Create realistic timetables.

Timetables should be established for the accomplishment of each phase of the program. All participants should agree upon the phases and all should be committed to meet them. Because it is not always possible to estimate how long it will take to accomplish many aspects of a plan, some flexibility should be there in the timetables and every effort should be made to make it reasonable to meet them.

4. Budget for the plan's implementation.

Making major changes, like every aspect of business, costs money. To ensure that your plan is cost-effective, a budget should be developed for the project. Carefully develop a reasonable estimate of what costs will be incurred.

5. Set forth a specific strategy to keep employees informed.

As all employees—not just the management group—are essential to a plan's success, it's important that periodic progress reports are published. These reports will keep the employees abreast of developments, accomplishments and modifications, if any, and will congratulate and thank people who were especially helpful.

> *Planning is the open road to your destination. If you don't know where you are going, how do you expect to get there?*
>
> Basil S Walsh

6. Establish a measurement system for the plan's success.

To track progress, a measurement system should be created. There are many such systems available. Research which system is most appropriate for the type of change involved and incorporate it into your plan timetables.

7. Include a process for continuing input.

Plans to make significant changes are dynamic. They are never truly final. As a plan is implemented, participants are likely to see new things, have new ideas and develop new approaches. Successful plans build in a process that encourages people to submit suggestions and recommendations.

> *The key to success is our ability to adapt. People underestimate their capacity for change. There is never a right time to do a difficult thing. A leader's job is to help people have vision of their potential.*
>
> John Porter

Augment Chances of Success

Because there is often resistance to trying something new, you need to bolster every step of your efforts to generate change. The following tips should help you in getting our change plan off the ground and keep it developing smoothly.

1. *Build a core team of leaders in the company.*

These individuals should be drawn from all ranks, not just the top management. Choose the natural leaders as well as those in highly influential positions such as plant supervisors.

In almost every organization there are men and women who may not have formal leadership positions but who play an important role in what goes on. They are often veteran employees who have gained the respect of their peers and who influence the others' opinions and actions. If you win their honest and wholehearted support, your chances of success are almost guaranteed.

The best way to obtain the support of these informal leaders is to involve them from the beginning. Identify and cultivate them early in the process and include them in the planning. Most importantly, maintain their confidences and never make promises to them you can't keep. Informal leaders are often loaded with ideas and suggestions on how to make things better. In a poorly run company, management often looks upon informal leaders who do not agree with them as enemies to be suppressed. This usually causes them to "go underground" and become persistent thorns in their boss's sides. Instead of perceiving them as troublemakers, these influential men and women should be looked upon as intelligent, capable people who have much to offer. Instead of opposing them, include them in the change process. Bring them in as full partners.

If the informal leaders are enthusiastic about what is happening, this will permeate the entire organization. By considering them as partners, you will have converted possible opponents to sincere proponents and in that way reverse the flow of energy. When this is compounded over dozens—perhaps hundreds—of employees, it can be a powerful element in achieving the success of the change.

2. *Communicate the importance of your vision.*

Make every employee responsible for the changes you will be implementing; your core team will simply be the role models. Explain how important this is to the company.

3. *Listen to the staff members.*

As discussed above, listening is essential to success, but you should to take it a step further. Hold meetings with all the staff, reassuring them that there will be no repercussions for anything negative that is said. Announce an open door policy and stick to it—listen to every idea that's presented without criticizing it.

4. *Ensure respect for individuals.*

The major problem with a dictatorial workplace is that employees feel a total lack of respect. After all, even the smallest decisions were made for them. To turn this around, begin with praise and encouragement. Let each individual know how much he or she contributes to the company; when there is a problem, make it seem easy to correct by taking the attention off the individual and focusing it on the system that created the problem.

5. *Create teams.*

Earlier, the staff was expeced to be workers. Now they're asked to be contributors. Create cross-functional work teams that meet to discuss and resolve problems that may arise. The staff members will not only begin to feel respected and valued, but they will also learn to trust their new co-workers. More on team building will be discussed in Chapter 5.

Of course, this is just the beginning. The most difficult challenge will be maintaining this new commitment to human relations as the company meets new crises. However, you must resist the temptation to revert to the old style of doing things. With perseverance, great rewards will result.

6. *Develop better than average competence.*

Darlene Thompson was intrigued by the new technologies in medical diagnosis and treatment. As a nurses' aid at Mercy Hospital, she observed but did not operate this new equipment. At every opportunity, Darlene went down to the department where this equipment was being used. She spoke to the technicians and was given literature she could study.

She was particularly interested in the use of the ultrasound machine, which is used to identify many internal disorders. Darlene enrolled in a training program, was certified as a Registered Diagnostic Medical Sonographer and was transferred to full-time work in this capacity. Most people obtaining this certification would be satisfied to get such a job but Darlene wanted to be more than just a good worker; she aimed to be the best possible technician. She continued her studies and volunteered to work on special projects with the physicians using the equipment. In a relatively short time, Darlene was the most technically knowledgeable sonographer in the hospital and was on her way to a successful career in this field. She hired two additional operators and had to train them. In order to assure that these trainees would be taught rapidly and efficiently, Darlene set up a training plan. The process of developing this plan forced Darlene to rethink many of the techniques that she had been using herself. She recalled some special approaches that she had not used in years and came up with some new ideas. Once the training began, the interaction between Darlene and the trainees stimulated her to improve her own performance and increase her personal productivity.

7. *Keep trying new ideas.*

Champions never say "It can't be done." They try to find a way to overcome the obstacles. Even champions don't always win, but they never lose without first making an effort to come out on top.

Norman Strauss, an industrial painting contractor in New York City, was faced with a major problem. His bid for the job of painting Madison Square Garden, New York's largest indoor sports arena, was due by the end of the week. The major problem was painting the ceiling, which was 110 feet above the first floor. The usual way of reaching the ceiling was to construct a pipe platform on which the painters would stand when they sprayed it. The cost of building the platform would be the same for all bidders. The only way to significantly reduce the bid would be to find some way to paint the ceiling of the building without building the pipe platform. Everybody knew this couldn't be done, so why bother?

But Norman Strauss did not give up easily. He believed that to achieve success one must never cease trying to solve a problem. On the way home that evening, Norman noticed an electric company repainting a high street light. To reach this light, they were using a cherry picker, a truck with an elevator on its roof that could be raised to various heights. “Why not use cherry pickers to reach the ceiling at the Garden?” Norman asked himself. His investigation the next day brought out that it was feasible and economical. Norman was able to submit a significantly lower bid than his competitors and got the job.

8. *Remember that training is an ongoing endeavor.*

Training does not stop when one has acquired technical competence. The best athletes continue to train no matter how successful they are. They know that the need for training never ends.

Sam Fredericks is a successful salesperson who does not believe he complains. Every year, Sam takes at least one training course in salesmanship or product knowledge. He schedules time every week to read books and listen to training tapes. This has resulted in Sam's continuing improved performance in servicing his customers and increasing his sales.

9. *Teach others to succeed at our new program.*

Another way to augment your chances of success is to teach others. Not only does this enable you to systematically review what you have been doing and reinforce it for yourself, but also you often learn from the trainee. Questions asked and suggestions made by the trainee can lead to more knowledge about one's own field.

10. *Fully plan the execution of the workplace change.*

Before commencing the job, it is essential that it be thought out. A superb performer thinks out how the job will be performed before beginning the project.

When instituting a change in any phase of your work, as much time must be given to the planning as to the work itself. Just as before making a sales call, the successful sales representative thinks carefully about all of the possible problems that may develop and how they can be handled, you must think about every ramification any aspect of the change may cause before making that change.

Learn from Successful Salespeople

No matter how competent you may be, unless you can sell your ideas to others, you may fall short of success. Whether it is persuading your boss to implement a suggestion you have made, your colleagues to cooperate on a project or your subordinates to put out more effort, your ability to "sell" is essential to your success. If you sincerely believe in what it is you are selling, it is not difficult to project that belief to others.

When Jennifer Deane, human resources director of the Sweet Sixteen Cosmetics Company, studied the company's time sheets, she saw that the need to do something about the increasing tardiness problem was critical. Punishment of latecomers had not helped and a plan to give awards to people with perfect records had not led to significant improvement. A year earlier she had suggested flextime as an alternative to the rigid schedule they had in place, but her boss had turned it down cold. How could she reintroduce this idea now and change his mind?

Selling ideas is not much different from selling a product or service. By following the approaches of successful salespeople, you can persuade people to accept your concepts. The first step in any sales activity is to be properly prepared. No good salesperson would attempt to make a sale without careful preparation.

Sales are contingent upon the attitude of the salesman—not the attitude of the prospect.

W Clement Stone

Clarify Your Ideas

Just as a salesperson must know his or her product thoroughly in order to be able to sell it, you must know as much as possible about the idea you want to sell. Before Jennifer even broaches the subject of flexible hours to her boss, she should know as much as she can about the feasibility and usual success of this concept. She should read the literature available about the subject, speak to executives at other companies that have adopted similar programs and feel out the attitudes of some of the employees who would be affected by it.

If there are variations of the concept you wish to present, learn about them and analyze these alternatives. Most ideas have drawbacks and limitations. Face up to them and know what they are and what steps must be taken to overcome them.

From your analysis of the subject, determine what this concept will do that no other concept is likely to do. In studying the experience of companies who use flextime programs, Jennifer learned that tardiness was reduced significantly in all of these firms. She also learned that the productivity did not suffer even though employees were not available at the same time. It also made recruiting of new employees, particularly parents of young children, easier. Jennifer presented her boss with the data she'd gathered and informed him that, "The outstanding feature of flexible hours is that it could combine these benefits—it will reduce tardiness without loss of productivity and at the same time attract good people to the company."

What's in It for the Buyer?

Every salesperson knows that the main concern of any buyer is: "What's in it for me?" How will the company benefit by accepting your idea? Most company executives are cost-conscious, so you must be able to demonstrate how your idea is cost-effective.

If you are selling the idea to a person with whom you work and know well, such as your immediate boss, you should know what his or her interests are. Prepare to tailor your presentation to these interests. If you can adapt what you offer to what the other person desires most, you have increased your likelihood of making the sale.

However, if the person to whom you are making your presentation is a virtual stranger, it is important to find out what is of real concern to that person. To learn this, you must be prepared to ask questions to uncover his or her real interests. From other people who deal with this person, find out all you can about him or her. You should try to meet with this executive before making the presentation and ask good questions that might enlighten you. Direct questions such as: "What do you wish to achieve in such and such an activity?" "What are your goals for this year?" or indirect questions such as: "What accomplishments in your past gave you most satisfaction? Why?" can help you prepare a sales pitch tailored to that individual. Listen carefully to the responses and you will pick up what it is that will really excite the buyer.

Developing Evidence

Good salespeople always have evidence available to prove their points. In selling an idea, the best evidence is the experience of other organizations that have used similar concepts successfully. Jennifer contacted several companies in her community that have offered flextime for several years and was able to obtain considerable data on the benefits they derived from it. She also found out what problems they had and how they overcame them. By learning about the negative aspects of flextime as well as the positive ones, she was able to prepare for objections that her boss might present.

Matching What You Offer With What Is Wanted

Facts alone will rarely make a sale. The salesperson must be able to show how those facts translate into benefits to the buyer. In preparing to sell an idea, list each of the facts that make your idea worthwhile in one column and next to them in another column, identify the benefit they provide the buyer.

For Jennifer's flexible hour concept:

Fact (What is Offered)	*Benefit (What is Desired)*
Reduce tardiness by 80%	Save $2,300 per month
Improve morale	Reduce turnover of staff
Attract better workers	Increase productivity

By showing how the idea you are selling will meet what the buyer wants for the company, your presentation will come across in a positive and persuasive manner. Nobody wants to be "sold." Everybody wants to feel that what has been bought is what he or she wanted to buy. By showing the person to whom you are presenting your idea how it fits into what he or she really wants, you are more likely to gain acceptance of the idea.

Now you are ready to make the presentation and sell the idea to the boss. How should the evidence by presented? If you know the person to whom you are selling the concept, you should know how they like to receive information. Some people may be more easily reached with charts, graphs and diagrams; others by cogent arguments or examples. By using the format that is most likely to impress your audience, you will have a greater chance of making the sale.

Get Attention

Salespeople often gain the attention of a prospect by commenting about the decor of the office or a picture on the wall or some other extraneous matter. When dealing with a person you work with, it is best to start with something you know will be of interest to that person. If he or she is "all business," then start right with the business at hand. "Doug, I know how concerned you have been about increasing productivity: One of the causes of this, as you know, is our difficulty in recruiting good support staff. If there were a way to attract more skilled people, you would want to know about it, wouldn't you?" The only response Doug could make is "Yes." Jennifer has presented the chief advantage of her concept and has gained immediate attention. She must now follow this up to determine Doug's specific interests.

Ask Questions and Listen to the Responses

Although from Jennifer's experience in working with Doug she knows much of what really interests him, she should be prepared to ask specific questions about his objectives. If you are dealing with a person whom you do not know well, this part of the presentation may be the most important. It is essential to uncover what is most important to this executive. You may learn that one person's major concern is cost-effectiveness, while another is more interested in how a new program or item affects his or her image.

Many people are so anxious to sell their ideas that they do not really listen to what the buyer really wants. Some salespeople assume that because the price of their product is lower than those of the competitors, they can emphasize cost savings, so they do not listen to the prospect's concern about quality. You should avoid presupposing that the executive's interests are the same as yours. Listen carefully to the answers to your questions and be prepared to pick up subtleties that can lead you to that person's real interests.

Presenting Evidence

In your preparation you should have developed considerable evidence to back up the ideas you wish to sell. Once you know what the executive to whom you must sell the concept really wants, you can tailor the evidence to that person's desires. Jennifer knows that her boss, Doug, is a pragmatist. He will not accept vague theories, but is impressed by facts and figures. She also knows he measures all projects on cost-effectiveness. To sell flextime to him, she must be ready to show him how it has worked in other companies and what it has cost.

"Doug, said Jennifer, "I discussed this with Hilary Hendricks, the human resources manager of Fitrite Shoes. They instituted flextime three years ago. She pointed out that it reduced tardiness by 80 percent, saving them $3,000 per month. In addition, the program has helped them recruit higher caliber support staff and has reduced turnover significantly."

Dealing with Objections

Salespeople like objections. It helps them determine what the prospect really wants and enables them to address that issue and increase their chances of making the sale. Good salespeople anticipate what objections are likely to be presented and are prepared to counteract them. You should know the most likely objections that your boss may have to the changes you are suggesting and be prepared to deal with them.

Doug turned down the concept of flextime the previous year because he felt that it would disrupt production. "If everybody comes in at different times, how can we coordinate production? Suppose the supervisor needs critical information from a worker who has already left or hasn't arrived?"

From Jennifer's research, she would have learned how other companies have coped with these situations and be prepared to point out how the advantages outweigh the limitations.

Closing the Sale

There are several approaches to closing a sale. One approach that is usually helpful in selling an idea to an executive is to ask him or her to help in evaluating your concept. Divide a paper into two columns. Name one column Negatives and the other Positives. Immediately list the major objections that have been brought up in the negative column and write the counteracting argument in the positive column. Add to the positive column all the additional benefits that have been discussed. If you have done your homework, you should have many more positives than negatives. Then ask, "If we look at some of the reasons that may cause us to hesitate to accept this idea and weigh them against the reasons in favor of going ahead, which side weighs heavier?" The answer has to be the positive side.

Once you have obtained agreement that the change you have suggested is viable, say, "As you agree this is a good idea, I would like to discuss how this can be implemented." If the change has to be sold by your boss to other executives before it can be adopted, suggest that you will be happy to assist in preparing for that presentation.

By careful preparation and by following the approaches used by successful salespeople, you can present and sell your ideas for change to your company and obtain the great satisfaction of being able to see those changes accepted and carried out.

> *The world hates change, yet it is the only thing that has brought progress.*
>
> Charles Kettering

When We Dislike the Assignment

From time to time everyone is given an assignment they dislike. There are many tasks incumbent to most jobs that are unpleasant, boring or tedious. Of course, that fact doesn't help too much when you have experienced the assignments you love and now have to take on something that isn't as much fun.

The key is to get through this time, to show that we're team players who are willing to do what's necessary. When your supervisor sees how well you perform a job that he or she knows you don't like, you will likely be rewarded with a more exciting assignment in the future. Keep that goal in mind as you work your way through this difficult time by using the following tactics:

Expect ingratitude.

Diane recently quit a job after 20 years with her company. The good-bye parties literally made her cry, not because she'd be missing her co-workers but because, for 20 years, she never realized how much they respected her and valued her work. "If only they'd given me some hint, I would have stayed," she lamented.

Unfortunately, ingratitude is common in the workplace. Many managers feel that since they're being paid, that's enough appreciation. We know that isn't true. Often a word of thanks is valued more than any monetary bonus, but we also can't change the system overnight. Realize that just because you were given this project, it does not mean you're being punished or that your past work wasn't valued. Unless the supervisor tells you otherwise, the two are unrelated.

Don't criticize, condemn or complain.

Dale Carnegie considered this a basic rule for good interpersonal relations. You may feel tempted to tell the world that you're being underutilized and feel your supervisor has made a mistake giving you this project.

You might even want to criticize the project itself, complaining that it's a waste of time and money. This will only serve to sustain your lack of motivation while giving you a bad reputation in the workplace. Even if you hate the assignment, now is the time to drop the subject and get to work.

We're Overqualified

You may feel that you are overqualified for some assignment. Instead of complaining, use this as an opportunity to bring a unique perspective that could save the company money or help you reach the deadline sooner. It may enable you to do the job in fewer hours, thus leaving free time to take on other projects. This may give you a chance to try new strategies you've always wanted to try on a project that would be best tested on something simpler. By showing this level of enthusiasm, you may find a new component to this project—it very well could be a proving ground for you, showing your supervisor that you have the skills and creativity to tackle more complex projects.

Coping with Changes We Reluctantly Accept

Cooperate with the inevitable

Everyone knows that we can't avoid or deflect change. It's a part of everything we do in our careers. When we remind ourselves of this we don't waste our time fighting the inevitable.

Do the very best you can

The most fundamental rule of business professionalism is to do the very best you can at all times. This motivates you internally, driving your efforts through whatever changes you are facing. Whatever way the change ends up impacting your career, you want to be able to say to others and to yourself that you did your very best.

Put enthusiasm into your work

How can you boost your enthusiasm about your work? How do I get motivated? What can I do to make sure that I am giving the most energy to my work as I can? Periods of change are times when you need as much enthusiasm as you can muster. You experience more enjoyment and sense of accomplishment from your work.

Staying Flexible during Change

Think of yourself as stretchable, expandable and able to adapt to anything new. Who wants to view themselves as static, inflexible and unable to adapt? Periods of change are unpredictable and you may be asked to adapt to changes that you never anticipated. In order to stay flexible, follow these guidelines:

- *Set short-term goals*

It is best during changing times to think ahead, but not too far ahead. Focus on goals and tasks that can be achieved in the immediate future. That way you can achieve measurable and motivating results, even if the plan is altered in some way. Instead of abandoning your efforts because of changing priorities, you complete your short-term goals and move on.

- *Work in intense bursts of activity*

Some people call this the "blitz mentality." Make a strong effort to complete tasks with intense periods of creative output that produce concrete results. That way you have measurable outcomes that motivate and inspire you to continue your work, and in the process better engage change.

- *Focus on team efforts*

Teams are in a constant state of changing responsibilities and deadlines. By aligning yourself with others who are aiming at similar goals, you create the opportunity for flexibility in achieving results. You become more focused on others and less likely to retreat into your own comfort zone. You gain motivation and inspiration from the other members of the team, making you more likely to successfully play a leadership role. We will discuss the role of the team in effecting change in Chapter 5.

• *Plan for possible change scenarios*

The most important strategy for staying flexible during change is to prepare for various change scenarios. If you create a plan for each possible set of change circumstances, you are prepared to engage change in any way that it affects you in the workplace. This gives you more flexibility, greater confidence and makes you more likely to be successful in leading the change without authority.

Sum and Substance

- A key factor for spurring yourself to success is the strong commitment you must have to strive for continuous improvement.
- To acquire credibility when suggesting change, you must perform your own job superbly. Obviously, if you are good in what you do, the boss is going to be able to depend upon you, making his or her job that much easier and making you that much more valuable to our organization.
- Don't be afraid to call the boss's attention to flaws and potential problems in his or her proposals. In this way, you provide a service that will not only result in better management on the part of the leader, but you also enhance

the likelihood that your original ideas and suggestions will be accepted.

- Before suggesting a change, think it out carefully. Consider not only it's positive values, but also evaluate all possible negative effects and be prepared to counter them.
- Even if you don't agree with changes instituted by the company, give them your best efforts and work to make them succeed.
- When you institute a change, you can augment your chances of it succeeding if the following steps are taken:
    1. Build a core team of associates from all echelons in the organization to support our efforts.
    2. Make sure that all aspects of the change are fully understood by all involved.
    3. Use all appropriate methods available to communicate your message to all involved.
    4. Encourage feedback from all participants.
    5. Create cross-functional work teams that meet to discuss and resolve problems that may arise.
    6. Train yourself on every aspect of the changes so you are thoroughly competent in implementing them.
    7. If obstacles arise, don't give up. Keep trying until a solution is found.
- No matter how competent you may be, unless you can sell your ideas to others you may fall short of success. Whether it is persuading your boss to implement a suggestion you have made, your colleagues to cooperate on a project, or your subordinates to put out more effort, your ability to sell is essential to your success. If you sincerely believe in what

it is you are selling, it is not difficult to project that belief to others.

- By careful preparation and by following the approaches used by successful salespeople, you can present and sell your ideas for change to your company and obtain the great satisfaction of seeing those changes accepted and carried out.

5

BE A TEAM PLAYER

Teams are not ends in themselves; they are a means by which to achieve other organizational goals.

Richard Wellins, William Byham, Jeanne Wilson

In today's workplace, we are expected to be contributing team players, often serving on several teams at once. Our ability to be seen as valuable members of these teams could have a significant effect on achieving our career goals.

Gaining a reputation as a valuable team member impacts your current work goals, your relationships at work, your opportunities for team leadership and the degree of satisfaction and motivation you feel in your job. It also can impact the degree to which a team embraces change. Each individual can have a significant effect on the success of change implementation.

In this chapter, we discuss the attitudes we project, the support we give to others during change, and the contributions we make to our work teams to help change succeed.

> *The key elements in the art of working together are how to deal with change, how to deal with conflict, and how to reach our potential . . . the needs of the team are best met when we meet the needs of individual persons.*
>
> Max DePree

Why Teams?

"Team spirit" is a term familiar to all of us. Since childhood in school and on the playing fields—we have been taught the value of working together to achieve our goals. Can we transfer this idea to the work place?

Today, most work must be done in groups. Very few jobs lend themselves to a single person working alone. If these work groups could be looked upon as teams, you might instill in the members of that group a feeling of belonging that leads to commitment and higher productivity.

In order to be an effective team player, it is helpful to understand how team leaders create and manage their teams.

Creating the Team

Dave was faced with a tough problem. His salespeople depended on the support of the office staff to obtain and maintain sales production. The salespeople were paid on a commission basis. They worked hard and long hours to get and keep accounts. They were often frustrated when the order department employees would stall deliveries by finding petty problems or the customer service representatives would antagonize a customer by indifference to an inquiry.

Dave divided the country into five regions and reorganized the departments into five teams, each one covering a region. Each team was made up of salespeople, order clerks, and customer service representatives and other support staff. In orienting them to the new system, Dave followed the T-E-A-M acronym for successful team development.

- *Train*

Before starting the new system, Dave brought all of his salespeople in from the field and held a weekend training program for the entire sales department. He explained how the program would work, how it differed from the current program and the advantages of working together to accomplish the goal of building and maintaining customers. Using discussion, role-plays and case situations, the group was trained to work together.

- *Enthusiasm*

To make any team activity work, the team members must not just accept the idea but greet it enthusiastically. Dave borrowed some of the techniques used in sports by having each team select a name and team color. He originally planned to pick names for each team, but realized it would be more empowering to allow each team to select it on their own. He announced that there would be contests between teams based on a variety of criteria, with awards ranging from group dinners to cash bonuses.

- *Assurance*

The teams were assured that they would not be left entirely on their own. Dave and other company executives would give them as much support as they needed in terms of advertising and promotion within specified budgets. Each team was assured that their ideas and concepts would be elicited and welcomed by top management.

- *Measurement*

Specific goals were set for each team and they were told how they would be measured. Performance reviews would be held as usual for each individual, but in addition to the usual measurements, how each person worked as a team member would also be considered. Bonuses and raises would be based on the team's productivity, encouraging team members to help each other.

At the end of the reorganization's first year, sales productivity had increased significantly. Instead of allowing orders to languish because of a minor error in the order form, the order clerks went to the source of the error and corrected it immediately. Secretaries and customer service representatives went out of their way to help the customers and the morale among all the sales and fulfillment staff was very high.

Working in teams has many advantages. People who learn to work together as a team will be more productive, will enjoy their work more and will be more likely to accept change. It will create a more motivational environment in the workplace and help build the esprit de corps that is so important for success in meeting goals.

Principles for Participating in Teams During Change

One way that you can contribute to your team during change is to keep your attitude positive and focused. These principles give you direction in keeping your attitudes centered on team success.

Team Members Should Support Each Other

During periods of change we sometimes feel like we are on a tightrope without a net. Even though other members of the team may be experiencing the same change, you may feel isolated and alone during organizational change. You must make a commitment to express support to everyone else on the team and let him or her know that the whole team is in this effort together. If you give unconditional support to your fellow team members, you will receive their support in return.

Have Fun

Let's face it. Sometimes we take ourselves a little too seriously. Sure, we are engaged in serious, demanding team efforts during periods of organizational change, but teamwork at its highest level is fast-paced, engaging and fun. Many of us feel that the most exciting and rewarding efforts in our work are team efforts. Let's make a commitment to make teamwork during change enjoyable and fun, rather than dreary and dull.

Find Efficiencies

One of the advantages of working on a team is that you can capitalize on the individual strengths of your team members. You don't have to do everything or even know everything when you are on a team. Focus on utilizing individual team member skills, experience and abilities to achieve a high level of team efficiency and accomplishment.

Build Competitive Team Spirit

You can take tremendous pride in being members of high-achieving teams. As you set and achieve goals, why not compete with yourself, push each other and your team to an ever higher level of performance? When you tap into your competitive spirit, you unite as a team and reach higher levels of success.

Think Big

Maybe the changes that you are undergoing as a team will be the best things that ever happened to each of you. Maybe you will come through the changes so successfully that you will achieve team recognition. Instead of viewing yourself as merely surviving the changes, let's think big and imagine the organizational changes as springboards to greater individual and team success.

> *Change your thoughts and you change your world.*
>
> Norman Vincent Peale

Communicate Expectations

The best way to break out of isolation is to communicate openly, honestly and often. What are your expectations of each other as a team? What are your expectations of the team effort and the results that you can produce? Commit to discussing these expectations and applying the highest levels of listening to one another. In this way, all members of the team can unite for a common purpose.

Sometimes it's difficult to communicate with some of your team members. We all have people in our lives that we don't particularly care for, but who we can't ignore. We also know the toll these relationships take on our own mental, and sometimes even physical health. We may dread having to be in the same room with these people. Worse yet, we may spend hours of precious time just dealing with the bad feelings we have.

It doesn't have to be this way. You don't have to like everyone on your team, but you can make challenging relationships easier on yourself by following a few key communication tactics:

1. *Begin in a friendly way.*

When Karl assessed his relationship with Todd, a member of his team, he reported: "Because I was uncomfortable with Todd, when I entered the room, I would sit as far away from him as possible, fold my arms and wait for the sparks to start flying. I never realized how this was making the situation worse until I made a conscious effort to smile at Todd and to ask him a personal question, such as how his family was doing or what he thought about the local football team's latest game. It didn't take long for our relation with each other to improve."

2. *Show respect for the other person's opinion.*

Never tell a person he or she is wrong. This can be difficult, especially if the person is antagonistic or poorly informed. When someone's suggestion is not appropriate or helpful, instead of criticizing the staff member, gently point out how it can be improved. Focus on the problem and the solution, not on the person involved.

3. *Try honestly to see things from the other person's point of view.*

Again, this can be a challenge when you are convinced that the other person is coming from a completely alien mindset. Yet, with a little practice, you can begin giving people the benefit of the doubt and start seeing why they might feel a particular way.

4. *Refrain from negative comments.*

Remember the old adage, "If you can't say something nice,

don't say anything at all." It may seem quaint, but it works, especially when we're in a contentious relationship.

Contributing to Team Relationships During Change

Teamwork is all about relationships. To effectively deal as a team with change, relationships on the team need to be trusting, supportive and respectful. When you'll follow these principles, you'll feel better about your fellow team members and yourself. Let's look at how some of Dale Carnegie's principles apply in this situation:

1. *Don't criticize, condemn, or complain.*

It's easy to find fault in others and the organization during the uncertainty of change. Change takes time to be successfully implemented. Instead of condemning the actions of others or boring people with your complaints, look for the strengths in others.

2. *Give honest, sincere appreciation.*

Focus on the traits you admire and appreciate in others. Focus on the aspects of the organization that inspire and motivate you. Express appreciation at every opportunity in order to avoid looking for faults.

3. *Accentuate the positive.*

When you are in the midst of change, are you the type of person who others want to work with, want to include and want to listen to? Or are you the opposite, someone who just makes everything more difficult? Look for ways to contribute to the process and motivate others.

4. *Show genuine interest in others.*

During times of change, many of us tend to withdraw into our own concerns. We become self-focused, anxious about the impact of the change on our careers. Instead, become interested in others, focus on them and learn from them.

5. *Smile.*

Smiling is one thing that you can control! You can commit to keeping a smile on your face and being someone that others enjoy encountering. A smile is the best way to exhibit confidence and friendliness during changing times. And, smiling is contagious. Create smiles for other people.

6. *Remember and use names.*

Remembering someone's naming is a way shows that the person matters. This is especially important during change, when people are often uncomfortable and feel that they are the only ones going through the change. Remembering and using names is a way you can create a connection to others and be supportive of the individuals on your team.

7. *Talk to others about their interests.*

By definition, you cannot become selfabsorbed when you focus on others. What are the interests of your team members? What could you ask them about their interests in order to get them to open up?

8. *Make the other person feel important, and do it sincerely.*

It's not uncommon to feel a little lost and unimportant when your work environment is shifting around you. If you feel this way, certainly others do as well. Take the time to let others on the team know that you think their contributions are important.

Levels of Listening

Nothing is more critical in teams during change than keeping open lines of communication. Of all the communication skills necessary to participating in effective teams, listening is the most important. Periods of change leave individuals with questions, observations and opinions that need to be heard within the team. The entire team benefits when individual team members believe that others on the team are listening to them.

In the energized, fast-paced environment of organizational change, we sometimes are not as focused on our listening skills as we need to be. Others on the team can perceive different levels of listening on our part. Our goal in looking at these levels of listening is to move ourselves up the levels to attentive and proactive listening within the team.

It's natural during times of change to be thinking and talking about your concerns and yourself much of the time. Many of us process these thoughts verbally in conversation with others. Challenge yourself to listen, instead. Encourage the other people in the organization to talk and see if you can be empathetic and understanding.

Be a good listener. Your ears will never get you in trouble.

Frank Tyger

Barriers to Team Success

A key change in many organizations is shifting to a team structure. The team can be a great boon to an organization. It can revitalize organizations that are going downhill; it can stimulate team members to become more creative and more productive. It can develop leaders for the future. But teams don't always work. Although, most companies report success in using them, there are a good many organizations in which shifting to teams has been disappointing. Some of the reasons for this are as follows:

Failure to Set Clear Goals

You cannot shift from work groups to teams by an edict from top management. You have to take the time to plan exactly what you want to do and how you intend to do it. Moreover, unless you know exactly what you want to achieve, there's no way to measure how close you are to achieving it. You must set specific goals as a standard against which progress can be measured.

The goals set for accomplishing the team's mission must be in line with the larger goals the company has established. If the objectives you plan to achieve for your job, department or team aren't coordinated with the objectives of the organization, you will waste your time and energy.

In most organizations, overall goals are established by top management and filtered down to departments or teams to use as guides in establishing their own goals. The process of setting goals takes time, energy, and effort. Goals aren't something you scribble on a napkin during a coffee break. You must plan what you truly want to accomplish, establish timetables, determine who will be responsible for each aspect of the job and then anticipate and plan resolutions for any obstacles that may threaten to thwart the achievement of the goals.

> *It is a paradoxical but profoundly true and important principle of life that the most likely way to reach a goal is to be aiming not at that goal itself but at some more ambitious goal beyond it.*
>
> Arnold Toynbee

Just as in initiating a plan for a change in the workplace, you have to diagnose the "as-is" situation before goals can be determined for your team. Too often, managers deceive themselves about the true condition of their organization. Of course, they know the figures: sales volume, market share, production, payroll and all the tangible statistics. But they often delude themselves on such vital information as employee attitudes and morale, the currency of the skills of their people, the willingness of their people to cooperate and extend themselves, the commitment of staff at all levels to company goals.

Each of us tends to accept as truthful information that which is compatible with our own perceptions. To us it is reality. However, in the minds of others, be they superiors, peers or subordinates, the same information may be perceived completely differently.

Just as in our bodies, many critical problems may not show up in routine tests; subtle and incipient conditions exist in an organization that may not be uncovered by traditional business analysis.

> *The manager who comes up with the right solution to the wrong problem is more dangerous than the manager who comes up with the wrong solution to the right problem.*
>
> Peter Drucker

You must go deeper and not rely on your suppositions. To do this we must get to know the people with whom you interrelate: members of the team, other team leaders and managers, and others within and outside the firm. You must learn their strengths and weaknesses, attitudes toward the job, the company and the leaders. Some companies accomplish this by employee attitude surveys, focus groups or using a special consultant to interview the staff. The "innerview" described in Chapter 2 is a powerful tool to obtain this information.

Poorly Conceived Organizations

To make teams work, the traditional hierarchical organizational structure has to be modified. Most companies have an organizational chart showing where each department fits in the company. It usually looks like a pyramid and your team may be somewhere near the bottom. The function of the organizational chart is to show staff associates which activities they are responsible for, to whom they report, and who reports to them. In addition, it enables anyone to view the entire corporate structure.

However, rigid adherence to this structure can impede the work of teams. Teams often cross structural lines. They don't fit neatly into a box. For example, a product-development team may engage in functions that fall under engineering, research and development, marketing and finance. Artificially placing it under the supervision could complicate its work.

Poor Leadership

Blame it on the boss! And often the boss is to blame. It's the team leader's responsibility to make the team succeed. No matter how competent the team members may be, unless they are guided by a knowledgeable, dedicated, inspiring leader, it will be tough for them to achieve their goals. If the leader doesn't lead, the team can't follow. Worse, if the leader leads badly, the team will perform badly.

Let's look at how one team leader abdicated his leadership role. When Rick D. was appointed leader of a marketing-development team, he studied books on team leadership, attended seminars and asked advice of other leaders. He was convinced that his team would be participative and that he would give his members enough autonomy so they could use their talents and grow by making decisions on their own.

When the team was assembled, Rick presented a broad outline of the team's purpose and asked them to determine what should be done and who would do it. When a member had questions about his role, Rick responded, "That's for you to determine."

Theoretically, that's how a participative team works. But what happened? Some members selected aspects of the project that they felt competent to do and began to work on it. Others spent weeks figuring out their roles; still others began working on part of the project only to find that somebody else was doing the same thing.

Without leadership, there was total confusion. It didn't take long for Rick's boss to note the lack of progress. When questioned about this, Rick responded that he was taught that giving team members autonomy would result in long-term benefits to all. What he failed to understand was that a project has to be completed in a structured fashion. If a team has never done a particular type of project before, it needs strong guidance from the leader, frequent feedback on progress, and active steps to keep the team moving on track. All this could be accomplished within the parameters of participative team leadership.

Inflexibility Toward Tasks

Another barrier to team success is improper understanding of the job description. In the traditional work group, the duties and responsibilities of a job are specified in a formal job description. Job descriptions have their place in the team setup, too. They give the members a guide to the work they are expected to perform, but all members are expected to do any work that will propel the team toward its goals.

Yet, there are invariably employees who look upon their jobs as being limited to the job description. When asked to help other members or to take on any assignment not specifically listed in the job description, they complain, "It's not my job."

The concept of the team is based on the principle that its members all work together to achieve the desired results. This means that all team members do whatever has to be done to accomplish the job. This includes doing work you don't enjoy, helping slower members catch up and putting aside pet projects to keep the team on target for higher priority assignments.

Lack of Trust

The basis for any relationship, on or off the job, is trust. When team members do not trust their leader or each other, the team will never get off the ground.

The success or failure of a team leader depends on the trust of his or her team. If people trust you, anything you say can be accepted. If people don't trust you, then most of what you say will be ignored.

It doesn't take much for a person to lose trust in another person. If the team leader makes a promise and then fails to live up to it, he loses his team members' trust. When a team member withholds needed information from other members, nobody trusts him or her again.

Rebuilding trust is not easy. If the lack of trust is among team members, the team leader can step in to alleviate the problem. However, if the team leader has lost the trust of the team members, it will take extraordinary effort to reestablish a trusting relationship.

> *If you treat an individual as if he were what he ought to be and could be, he will become what he ought to be and could be.*
>
> Johann Wolfgang von Goethe

Poor Distribution of Work

Sandra was mad. Once again the team was behind schedule and that meant she would have to work overtime. And whose fault was that? Not hers. She knocked herself out to get the work done on time, but some of her teammates, like Carl and Tricia, just plodded along. When she complained to Chloe, the team leader, she was told that they were doing the best they could.

An inequitable distribution of the workload among team members is not an unusual situation. True, some people work more quickly than others, some are more thorough than others, and some are more creative than others. We could argue that it's human nature for the Sandras of this world to resent the Carls and Tricias who, in their opinions, are not contributing as much to the team effort as they are. This resentment is exacerbated when the Sandras have to make up for these deficiencies by doing extra work.

No team can succeed unless every member does his or her share. The team leader cannot accept the excuse that Carl and Tricia are doing their best. She has to identify the reasons for their poor performance and take steps to correct it. Perhaps they need additional training; perhaps they have personal problems that are impeding their performance.

Lack of Ownership

Employees who have been accustomed to working in traditional settings have been conditioned to taking orders. For years, they were excluded from the decision-making process. As team members they feel uncomfortable when asked to participate in decision making and in taking ownership of their work.

Often they've been told that one reason supervisors and managers were paid more than rank-and-file workers was they had the responsibility of making decisions. Now, as team members—not paid any more than before—they are given this responsibility. It's logical for them to feel that making decisions is not their job.

In most companies, team leaders do get a higher base pay than team members, but this should be an incentive for team members to aspire to be promoted and should result in their being less reluctant to participate in decision making.

> *If you want to build a ship, don't drum up people together to collect wood and don't assign them tasks and work, but rather teach them to long for the endless immensity of the sea.*
>
> Antoine de Saint-Exupéry

Poor Communications

Another reason that teams fail to work is a breakdown in communications. You say one thing and your associate hears something quite different. Why? It could be how you said it, or how the associate received it. Trite as it may sound, poor communication is a major barrier to the success of team efforts.

You thought your instructions were clearly stated. But the minute you leave the room, one associate turns to another team member for clarification. Why? Maybe it was your fault. Perhaps you spoke indistinctly. Perhaps you used language that was not familiar to the listener. Perhaps your body language sent a different message from your words. Maybe the problem originated with the associate. He didn't fully listen. She didn't take you seriously.

Whether you are the team leader or a team member expressing your views, you have to be alert as to how you come across to others. Get feedback from your associates. Ask them for critiques on your presentations at meetings or just in team discussions. If you are making a planned presentation, rehearse it in front of a mirror or videotape it.

> *Perception is in the mind of the perceiver. Unless the leader's perception and team member's perception of a situation are congruent, they will be working at cross purposes.*
>
> Arthur R Pell

Be a Coach

Good leaders are good coaches. A manager can tell people what to do and when to do it, but only a good coach can motivate them to give the job their full attention. Others may point out problems, but a coach is there to help solve those problems. Many in leadership positions will hold a carrot out for people to go after. But a coach will motivate the individual to want to give the best performance possible.

Some people are natural coaches. But most of us can learn and put into practice the elements of coaching used by successful coaches.

Get to Know Team Members

When coaching an individual, it is very helpful to tune in to him or her at a personal level. Get to know the individual better. By using the "innerview" technique described in Chapter 2, find out about the person's family situation and the high points and low points in their lives. Find out how they survived low points that they encountered in school, in personal activities and of course, in their jobs.

John Ralston, an NFL football coach for the Denver Broncos, encouraged his coaching staff to do just that. They'd ask a few questions to a player on the way to the field and back to the locker room. They then used these answers to motivate each player in individual ways. They won the Rose Bowl twice in a row.

Build Self-Esteem

Often what you have to coach your team about relates to allaying fear and building self-confidence. Encourage people by telling them how much their work is valued.

Ask Insightful Questions

Greg, a top-tier sales manager reported, "After making sales calls with my sales reps, I'd ask for the three things they did well on the call and one area that could be improved. Then I'd suggest how they could do even better in the areas in which they did well and how to improve in the area that needed improvement."

Don't Avoid Those Who Resist

A management consultant recently helped facilitate a meeting of managers who wanted to work more effectively as a team. The consultant reported: "We looked at all the barriers to working better together and then worked on the easiest ones first. When it got to the most difficult concern, we decided to put together a committee. I asked the most resistant person on this issue to be a member of the committee. Not only would he be a strong advocate of a negotiated solution but because he had a different viewpoint, he could provide a great deal of insight."

Don't Pretend to Be Perfect

As a leader, there are times you need to criticize, but there are ways to make that work. You can build rapport. Relate similar issues you faced and talk about how you resolved them. Reassure the team member that although he may have faltered, he isn't a bad person.

Believe in What You Do

Coaching is hard work. It's rarely given the limelight. Yet, by being a strong coach, you can move your team to work wonders while giving individuals the sense of accomplishment they need.

Some additional techniques that will improve your coaching are:

- Praise and recognition
- Positive feedback techniques
- Recognizing people's strengths, as well as, accomplishments
- Discussing appraisals
- Discussing performance
- Discussing interpersonal relationship issues
- Counseling
- Feedback
- Participation in policy development
- Special work assignments and projects
- Management seminars
- Specialized training courses
- Case study discussions
- Attendance at conferences and meetings on technical or management subjects
- General administration (executive) training courses

Encourage the Team to Initiate Change

A progressive team should always be on the alert to determine when and where changes can be made—to seek opportunity to improve the "as-is" situation. There are five ways in which new opportunities might be identified:

1. Team members identify an opportunity for themselves.
2. Team members identify an opportunity for another person.
3. A customer, vendor or outsider identifies an opportunity.

4. The team leader identifies new skills needed within the team.
5. A situation creates an opportunity.

These different opportunities may arise due to a new need, taking on a new job or a project that requires a new skill, in the course of a performance review, after a mistake occurs or in connection with some other event.

Once the opportunity is identified, it is important to take the time to pinpoint what the situation will look like when the gap is filled. This is a step that many people skip or don't develop fully, which can lead to confusion, misunderstanding and frustration for all involved.

One of the most important concepts in coaching team members to utilize these opportunities and take the necessary steps to initiate change is having a vision or end goal in mind. Without good coaching, people often lose sight of the importance of making the needed changes. People with a clear vision of the end result of coaching tend to move in that direction more quickly than those without. But, it is critical that both the coach and the trainee own the goal. Without that sense of ownership, motivation may be lost. We focus on motivation and buy-in even more in the next step of the process, but this is where direction and motivation really begin.

Use encouragement. Make the fault seem easy to correct.

Dale Carnegie

In order for the coaching process to be successful, it is important that the appropriate resources be available. This includes time, money, equipment, training, information and most importantly, a personal commitment to succeed by all involved. Essential to this is the buy-in and support of the upper levels of management.

The team leader must ensure that the appropriate resources are in place and available. Nothing is as frustrating as being promised something and then not getting it. It can make everyone feel like they have been set up to fail.

Once the resources are in place and the correct skill set has been identified, explained and demonstrated, it is now time for the team members to practice and apply what has been learned. In order for knowledge to evolve into a skill, practice it and perfect the skill using the best techniques of coaching, to ensure that you are practicing the new skill and not the old habit.

Practice also allows the coach to identify strengths and opportunities for improvement. Some of the points to consider here are:

- How to encourage others to succeed?
- How closely to monitor others and when to let go?
- How to hold others accountable for progress?

Making progress is one thing, but without a way to reinforce it and keep it in place, people may quickly go back to the way they did things before. One of the biggest fallacies managers hold on to is the assumption that if people know how to do something, they will do it. People don't do what they know; they do what they have always done.

Some of the skills you must use in reinforcement of coaching are:

- Empowering people to get results after they have learned new skills.

- Giving the right kind of feedback.
- Following up with team members.
- Handling nonperformance issues.
- Handling mistakes and people who get off track.

One of the best ways to cement growth and progress is to reward it. What you reward gets repeated. What gets repeated becomes habit.

Change is uncomfortable. That is why people often revert back to their former ways quickly, if reinforcement and reward are not there. Habit is stronger than knowledge. To ensure change happens quickly and is kept in place as long as needed, celebration and reward are important. Hailing team members' success is a great way to encourage them to remain steady in the change or changes that have been made and to take the reins when it comes to generating new ideas and taking risks.

> *Individual commitment to a group effort—that is what makes a team work, a company work, a society work, a civilization work.*
>
> Vince Lombardi

Self-Development

Management should encourage staff members to take steps to improve their strengths and overcome their limitations. A ambitious person would take these steps on his or her own even if the organization does not encourage it or pay the costs.

Some of these self-improvement actions are:

- Holding office in civic organizations and professional societies

- Participating in community affairs
- Committee work
- Attending, participating in and organizing conferences, conventions, workshops, symposia, and institutes
- Writing articles

Sum and Substance

- One way that you can contribute to your team during change is to keep your attitudes positive and focused. This approach keeps you centered on team success.
- Instead of viewing yourself as merely surviving the change, let's think big and imagine the organizational change as a springboard to greater individual and team success.
- Teamwork is all about relationships. To effectively deal as a team with organizational change, relationships on the team need to be trusting, supportive and respectful.
- Of all the communication skills necessary to participating in effective teams, listening is the most important. Periods of change leave individuals with questions, observations and opinions that need to be heard within the team. The entire team benefits when individual team members believe that others on the team are listening to them.
- Before goals can be determined for your team, you have to diagnose the "as-is" situation. Too often, managers deceive themselves about the true condition of their organization.
- The team leader has the responsibility to make the team succeed. No matter how competent the team members may be, unless they are guided by a knowledgeable, dedicated, inspiring leader, it will be tough for them to achieve their goals.

- The concept of the team is based on the principle that its members all work together to achieve the desired results. This means that all team members do whatever has to be done to accomplish the job.
- The success or failure of a team leader depends on the trust of his or her team. If people trust you, anything you say can be accepted. If people don't trust you, then most of what you say will be ignored.
- Whether you are the team leader or a team member expressing your views, you have to be alert as to how you are perceived by others. One way to do this is to get immediate feedback from your associates.
- One of the most important methods of assuring success when making changes is coaching team members to utilize new opportunities and take the necessary steps to initiate changes. Without good coaching, people often lose sight of the importance of making the needed changes.
- In order for the coaching process to be successful, it is important that the appropriate resources be available. This includes time, money, equipment, training, information and most importantly, a personal commitment to succeed by all involved.
- Management should encourage all team members to take steps to improve their strengths and overcome their limitations. This will result in greater self-confidence and in turn, greater innovation and acceptance of change.

6

REDUCING STRESS DURING THE CHANGE PROCESS

In Chapter 3, we learned how to adjust to changes in the workplace. Many people suffer from stress during times of change. If you are among this group, there are steps you can take to alleviate the stress and cope with the changes.

In this chapter, we examine some of the factors that contribute to creating stress, and how we can reduce worry and stress by changing our approach to the situation.

What Is Stress?

According to the American Institute of Stress there is no definition of stress that everyone accepts. As there's no agreement on what exactly stress is, it's difficult to measure it.

Although, people have very different ideas with respect to their definition of stress, a common definition is: "physical, mental, or emotional strain or tension." Another popular definition of stress is: "a condition or feeling experienced when a person perceives that demands exceed the personal and social resources the individual is able to mobilize."

Most people consider stress to be something that causes distress. However, increased stress often results in increased productivity and accordingly stress is not always a negative experience. A definition of stress should also embrace this often-ignored "healthy stress."

Hans Selye, an early authority on stress, used the term eustress for "good" stress, such as winning a race or an election. Achieving a goal may be just as stressful as not achieving it. Making a successful presentation to top management may be as stressful as having our idea rejected. Any understanding of stress should include both eustress and distress.

The aspects of stress that most people tend to focus on are the negative feelings and emotions it produces. Almost every description of stress also discusses certain resultant physical, physiological or biochemical responses that are experienced or observed.

In most jobs, from time to time periods of stress develop. Stress may be generated by efforts to meet deadlines, to advance, to please a tough boss or by some other vicissitude of the workplace. During periods of change in some aspect of our jobs, most of us feel added stress.

Coping With Stress

What is most helpful to you when you feel overwhelmed by stress? As noted above, stress is not necessarily bad. Stress often motivates one to accomplish things that seem impossible to achieve. However, when stress becomes too great to handle, it can lead to physical and psychological impairment.

> *Adopting the right attitude can convert a negative stress into a positive.*
>
> Hans Selye

Fortunately, it is possible to cope with most stressful situations by applying one or more of the stress reducers listed in the acronym, "STRESS."

S elf-Awareness
T ender Loving Care
R elaxation
E xercise
S ense of Humor
S eek Help from Others

Self-Awareness

Ben's temper had caused him innumerable problems in his life. He had a short fuse and whenever he was the slightest bit stressed, he would scream at whoever was near him. It would relieve the immediate tension in him—but cause tension in all the people around him.

When Ben was cautioned by his boss that his future in the company was in jeopardy if he could not keep his temper under control, he realized that he needed to better understand his outbursts of anger. Ben tried an experiment with himself—for the next week, whenever his children started fighting with each other, he didn't immediately break up the fight with angry words. He paused and calmed himself and in a normal tone of voice asked his children to discontinue their tiff. He learned that what he'd considered a stress reliever—getting the stress out of his system by ranting and raving—was not only causing problems with other people, but was actually exacerbating his own stress. This awareness led to a concerted effort on Ben's part to contain his emotional outbursts.

Ben made a game out of this new behavior and he built up his resistance to give in to bursts of anger. Not only did he reduce his tantrums, but he more readily accepted the matters that had caused the outbursts, reducing the stress of his job.

> *Stress is not what happens to us. It's our response to what happens. And response is something we can choose.*
>
> Maureen Killoran

Tender Loving Care

Taking care of oneself is important for good health and people in good health are less likely to be stressed. Beverly was overweight, had slightly elevated blood pressure and always seemed to be tense. Everything annoyed her and she had frequent headaches and other physical problems. She always looked bedraggled and paid little attention to her clothes and appearance. She blamed all her health problems and her disregard for her appearance on the pressures of her job. Her physician persuaded her that the opposite might be true: her poor self-care was affecting her experience of her work. She agreed to go on a diet in order to lose weight and lower her blood pressure. The result: she lost weight, felt healthier, and started to take more interest in her appearance. She was inspired to change her hairstyle and buy some new clothes.

By treating herself with tender, loving care, Beverly became less tense and was able to cope with many of the aspects of her job that had previously stressed her.

Nothing is stronger than habit.

Ovid

Relaxation

Most stress experts agree that when one is under stress, relaxation is the most effective immediate therapy. How one relaxes depends on the circumstances in which the stress occurs and the different methods of relaxation appropriate for the individual and the situation.

When a group of men and women were surveyed on what they did to relax, some of the responses were:

- Window shopping
- Yoga exercises
- Meditation
- Deep-breathing exercises
- Going outside and getting some fresh air
- Working on a different assignment for a while

Each of us should develop several relaxing activities that can be appropriately engaged in on the job. Even a few relaxing moments can reduce our stress and enable us to return to the job refreshed and ready to deal with it.

The time to relax is when you don't have time for it.

Confucius

Exercise

Exercise helps to release tension and enhance our mood. Steve, a money manager in an investment firm, had to make decisions every day that could make or lose millions of dollars for his company. He came home from work so stressed that he would yell at his children and fight with his wife. It reached the point where his children would hide when they heard his car coming in the driveway. At the advice of a counselor, he joined a health club. Instead of going straight home after work, Steve now plays a hard game of racquetball at the gym. By the time he gets home all the tension is out of his system and a wholesome family life has been reestablished.

Sense of Humor

When the pressures are beating us down, it is hard to see any humor in a situation. However, when we look back at things that have stressed us in the past, we often laugh at them.

Karen's boss had just chewed her out. Sure, she had misinterpreted his instructions and made a major error in the project, but he should have recognized that if his instructions had been clearer, this wouldn't have happened. At first, she was tense, unhappy and felt unfairly treated. However, instead of letting these bad feelings dominate the rest of her day, she reminded herself that her boss often overreacted and that his temper problems were his problems, not hers. "Didn't he look silly with his red face?" she thought. She began to laugh. The stress began to fade as she tackled the job of correcting the project.

Seek Help from Others

Sometimes stress is so overwhelming one cannot cope alone. Professional counselors, clergy and specialists in specific areas can be called upon to help. When Judith's husband died, she was so distraught she could not do her job. Fortunately, she had the good sense to seek help from a grief therapist, who helped her cope with the situation. Regardless of the "size" of our problem (from the loss of a loved one to a perceived slight by a friend), we should consider seeing a professional counselor at any time that the stress in our lives is too challenging to manage.

Reducing Stress By Controlling Our Attitude

Often your stress is either caused or increased by your attitude toward the situation you face or the changes that are being instituted. You may be worried about whether you have the skills needed to perform certain work and the possibility of making serious errors. In the Dale Carnegie seminars, participants are shown some ways to overcome these worries:

Focus on the Present

Don't worry about the past and don't focus on the future. You can't change the past. You can't change what others will think—or say—about you because of past mistakes. You must forgive yourself and attend to what needs attending now.

Much of the work stress comes from worries about events that either have already occurred or that you fear may occur in the future. Relatively little of your day-to-day work stress stems from today's activities. As a ship has compartments that can be sealed to prevent water in one compartment from flooding another, you need to seal off the past and the future. You will accomplish more today by concentrating on today's problems than you will by brooding about the past or worrying about the future. Carnegie points out that 90 percent of our worries are over situations that have already occurred or that may or may not occur in the future.

Carnegie cautioned: "We can be content to live the only time we possibly can—today." Indeed, many of our day-to-day worries come from illogical fears of outcomes that are not likely to occur. If the odds are that the dreaded result will not occur, we do ourselves a service by setting the worry aside and moving on. Dale Carnegie referred to this principle as putting a "stop-loss order" on a stressful situation, just as an investor might do with a stock purchase. Sure, there will be setbacks from time to time. When that happens, cut our losses and continue on.

Be Our Best Selves

Often when we feel insecure we start to mimic the behavior of others. All too often, that is the beginning of a series of events that eventually turn destructive. We can't be someone else. We can't relate to the manager the same way our coworker does. We can't land a sale the same way our manager landed one last year. Instead, when looking at how to handle a new situation, turn to your instincts. Certainly listen to the advice you are being given, but manipulate it into a format that works for you. You should excel at being the best you can be while being who you are. Analyze your own mistakes and criticize yourself in ways that are constructive. Try to figure out why you may have made certain mistakes and then develop a plan for solving the problem. To reduce stress, you should check in with yourself about the quality of life you are living. You don't have to climb to the top of every mountain. If you don't want a high-pressure job, you should allow yourself to look into less stressful positions.

Be Realistic About Your Workload

Taking on more work than you can successfully perform is a surefire way to enhance your stress. If you feel your manager requires more than is feasible, discuss the problem and try to reach an equitable solution.

Count Your Blessings

It is always advisable to count your blessings and not your troubles. In a world fraught with war, famine, disease and natural disaster, a failure on the job is not the worst thing that can happen. Keep a list of all your blessings in your wallet or purse. Include on it your family, friends, health, talents, and the like. Then, when you're feeling stressed or like a failure, take it out and be thankful for having all the gifts and advantages you enjoy. You were successful many times in the past. You won't feel better by putting too much energy into the things that went wrong or the things you don't have.

Appreciate Others

You can reduce the stress you feel by simply turning your attention away from yourself. When the office feels overwhelming, you can pause and appreciate your coworkers. As much as you sometimes feel that way, you really would not like everyone else to be just like you in the workplace.

It would be boring. Differences in backgrounds, perspectives and work styles make the workplace more interesting and vibrant, not less. Work on appreciating the unique strengths in others. More on this will be discussed in Chapters 7 and 8 in this book.

Follow Good Work Habits

Following good work habits keeps you focused on the issues that require your attention. Clear the desk of all papers except those relating to the immediate problem at hand. Then, make a list every morning, prioritizing the day's activities with the most important tasks to be completed first.

When a problem arises, solve it immediately, if possible. If the facts necessary to make a decision are not fully available, decide whether to put it off until a definite date when you have the facts or to delegate the fact-gathering. This principle points to another productive work habit. Instead of putting off decisions and actions, dive in and start making positive results happen. You feel like you are making more forward, fruitful progress when you get moving and keep busy in a constructive way.

It is easy to get bogged down in minor details when facing challenges in your professional life. Focus on the big picture and let go of the trifles.

> *Being busy does not always mean real work. The object of all work is production or accomplishment and to either of these ends there must be forethought, system, planning, intelligence, and honest purpose, as well as, perspiration. Seeming to do is not doing.*
>
> Thomas Alva Edison

Delegate

A common trap many employees fall into is doing the work themselves when they're short-staffed. However, it's your job to make sure the work gets done, not to take on every task yourself. Look at the tasks you can easily share with others and if appropriate, delegate them.

Go With the Flow

No matter how carefully you prepare and plan, it is inevitable that mistakes occur, goals fall short or people fail to meet our expectations. Losing control of your emotions over these inevitable occurrences only makes matters worse. The more productive work habit is to "go with the flow" and cooperate with the situation.

Leave Work at the Workplace

Earlier in this chapter several ways to build relaxation into your workday were noted. You must also learn to relax at home. While your job is important, so is your health and family life. You cannot be effective at work or in your private life if we're feeling overwhelmed. A good practice is to schedule time with your family. No matter what the problems at work, this family time takes precedence.

Reducing Stress by Problem Solving

When a problem arises at the workplace, you often feel your stress levels rise. By taking a deliberate approach to problem solving, you can both handle the issue before us and keep your stress under control. Dale Carnegie suggests this three pronged approach when faced with problems on the job:

- Get all the facts.
- Weigh all the facts, and then come to a decision.
- Once a decision is reached, act!

These three principles connect together to form a comprehensive, organized approach to facing troublesome situations. Gathering all the facts before jumping to conclusions gives us a better basis for making decisions. Careful analysis and weighing of the facts give us more reliable decisions and taking action sooner, rather than later, allows us to move on.

Problems are only opportunities in work clothes.

Henry Kaiser

Solving problems is an important part of most management jobs. Supervisors must deal with problems concerning operations, production, quality, personnel and sometimes marketing and financial areas. It is common for managers to deal with these problems as they had in the past. If they have been involved in the type of work for any length of time, the chances are that similar problems have arisen previously. By applying what worked before, there is a good possibility it will work again.

Unfortunately, previously used solutions do not always have the same positive result. Although, the problem appears to be the same as before, circumstances may be somewhat different. To avoid this situation, make sure just what the problem really is before trying to tackle it.

Get All the Facts

A major manufacturer of refrigerators had lost a significant share of its market to a competitor. In the past, when market share had decreased, the reason for it was increased advertising on the part of the competitor involved and the manufacturer overcame it by increasing its own advertising. Using this past experience as a guide, the staff developed a good advertising campaign to overcome the current loss. To their surprise, the advertising did not help at all—in fact, the market share continued to decrease.

Further study showed that this time the competitor had not done any unusual advertising, but had increased the markup given to the retailers. This gave the retailer added incentive to push the competitor's product, even when the customer visited the store as a result of the manufacturer's own enhanced advertising. They had tackled the wrong problem. Study the problem—it may not be as it first appears.

Often when you seek the cause of a problem, you see only the tip of the iceberg. The problem is much deeper. You have an itchy rash. The dermatologist prescribes a salve, which you apply. The itching stops; the rash goes away. You think you have solved the problem. But two weeks later it returns. What has happened? The doctor treated the symptom—the rash. True, the rash was a real problem to you, but it was not the real cause of the problem, which might have been an allergy or another medical situation. To find the real cause or causes of the problems in your job, you must look for the critical factor(s) from which the problem has arisen. This requires a detailed study and careful analysis.

I have learned that success is to be measured not so much by the position that one has reached in life as by the obstacles which he has overcome while trying to succeed.

Booker T Washington

Typically, when faced with a problem, you may think of an immediate solution and rush it into effect. Just because a possible solution comes to mind immediately, it does not mean that it is the best solution. It is far better to consider a variety of possible solutions before choosing the one to be tried.

Keep an open mind. Seek suggestions from the people who are closest to the problem, particularly members of your staff who work with the situation and will be involved in implementing the action that will be taken. Call on experts in the company (or outside the company, if appropriate) to benefit from their experience and knowledge. Be creative—you are often more creative than you realize. By utilizing this often hidden power within us, innovative concepts can be uncovered that may solve your problems.

Weigh All the Facts and Then Come to a Decision

Once several alternatives have been developed, weigh all the factors and decide which solution is the best. To do this, it is necessary to review the problem and determine what the solution chosen must accomplish if the problem is to be solved.

List those items that are absolutely essential to the solution. These may include maximum cost, time limitations, use of personnel and other resources. Then list those items that are not essential, but would make the chosen solution even better.

When the New Wave Hairdressers were seeking a new location, they listed several factors as essential for the new business's home:

- The new location must be in an active shopping mall.
- It should be no less than 7000 square feet.
- The monthly rent must be no more than "x" dollars.
- The space must be available within the next six months.

Nonessential, but preferential factors included:

- There was 8500 square feet for the same amount of rent.
- The landlord would pay for redecorating costs.
- There were no other hairdressers in the mall.
- There were some high-fashion boutiques in the mall.

New Wave should not even consider a location unless all of the essential factors are met. Then, by weighing the various preferential factors, the owners can determine which is the best deal for them.

Once a Decision is Reached, Act!

Once a decision is made, put it into effect. Each person involved in implementing the solution should be assigned his or her part, resources should be assembled and the action started. As a supervisor, you should be on top of the situation. If there are some people on the staff who are not enthusiastic about the solution, you should point out the advantages to them. Be available to help those involved to understand what has to be done and to demonstrate where appropriate.

There are times when the type of problem involved requires a solution to which the company must commit itself for extended periods (e.g., moving to a new location). If the solution chosen does not work, there is little one can do to salvage it. Therefore, in such situations, the problem analysis must be performed with utmost skill. Fortunately, most problems faced by supervisors do not have irreversible ramifications and can be revisited if they do not work.

When putting such a solution into effect, ask: "How long will it take to determine if this solution is working?" Then set a follow-up date accordingly. At that time, evaluate what has occurred and if it has not solved the problem, drop it and select one of the other alternatives. There is no reason to stick with a solution that is not effective when there are other options available.

Reducing Stress By Controlling Our Time

When people are asked what causes them to be stressed, one of the first responses is "There isn't enough time to do what must be done." Careful management of our time can minimize this problem by allowing you to be (and perhaps as importantly, to feel) more productive.

> *Time is what we want most, but what we use worst.*
>
> William Penn

Your work for the day had been carefully planned and nicely scheduled. Now the day is over and only a fraction of what you had planned to accomplish has been done. Where did the time go?

It's likely you tackled the projects on your calendar with the full intention of completing them, but no sooner had you started when you were hit by one or more of the plagues that steal away your time. There are dozens of these time robbers, a large portion of which take the form of interruptions. Let's look at a few of the most common plagues and what you can do to minimize their effects.

Our Computers

If you work at a desk you undoubtedly have a computer in front of you all day. This means that you're always receiving e-mails and have access to the Internet and any social media sites that you may be active on. Clearly, this volume of input and distraction can serve as a rabbit hole of valuable time. (Of course, your employers would prefer that you not spend our time at work shopping online and checking your personal e-mail messages and your Facebook page. If you must do so, you should make it your practice to only engage in these activities during your break time.)

In many workplaces today, nearly all communication occurs through the office's computer network. Constantly interrupting your work to read e-mails and the like causes one to lose significant productivity, both in time spent on the interruption itself and in time spent refocusing on the interrupted task.

We recommend making a point of reading your e-mails and instant messages at regular, scheduled intervals, rather than perpetually switching back and forth between tasks. Not only do you get more work accomplished (diminishing your stress), but you also take control of the way your time is spent. Being in a reactive situation at work (where you must consistently respond to needs, like a customer service representative) is considered by many to be more stressful than being in a proactive situation at work (where you determine what you will do when). If your e-mail makes a noise whenever you get a new message, have a tech support staff member turn that feature off. Something as small as setting aside time to read and respond to office messages can go far in eliminating the stress you experience during the work.

The Telephone

You're sitting at your desk deeply engrossed in your work and the phone rings. It is a colleague with a business question. But does this colleague get right into the business? Not usually. He or she will chat about the weather, his weekend activities or her vacation plans before starting the discussion. While the phone is used less frequently than it once was (at least for making calls), phone calls can take up an unnecessary amount of your work time. The time spent on most business calls could be shortened significantly if one concentrated only on the business at hand. However, to eliminate all personal chitchat would have negative effects as well. A little social conversation eases the relationships between people and helps develop a more pleasant work environment, resulting in more cooperation and teamwork. It is possible to be socially appropriate and yet keep the call brief. If the caller persists in lengthy unrelated discussions, politely say: "I'd love to hear more about that party, but I have a deadline to meet," and then move onto the business aspect of the conversation.

When you initiate a call, one of the major time robbers is waiting when the person you call is speaking on another call. Unless it is an urgent matter, leave a message on that person's voicemail briefly stating the matter and suggest response by return call, e-mail or personal visit.

If you feel it is important to wait, use these two, three, five minutes or more constructively. You could accomplish a fair amount of work while holding. Clerical detail work, record keeping, scanning mail or e-mail are some of the tasks you can do while waiting to speak. For a person who makes many calls each day, constructive use of just three minutes waiting time on ten calls adds a half-hour each day of productive time.

Visitors

You look up from your desk and at your door stands Loquacious Lou. You just don't have the time to listen to Lou's litany of pet peeves. It is not necessary to invite Lou in. Stand up. Walk in front of the desk, blocking off Lou's route to the guest chair and talk to him while standing. People tend to be much briefer when they have to stand than when they sit. If his message is important and work-related, you can always invite him to sit down. If not, guide Lou gently out of the door.

Marge, a freelance writer, works out of her home. For a while, one of her neighbors visited her every morning to chat. Marge did not have the time for coffee-klatches. Although, she enjoyed the social contact, she recognized that unless she stopped these visits, she could not accomplish her writing projects. A heart-to-heart talk with the neighbor explaining her need for time to work solved this without jeopardizing their friendship. People do understand that time is finite, but sometimes they have to be reminded of our time constraints, and that you must use your time optimally.

Paperwork

Although electronic communications and documents have replaced the overwhelming volume of papers most workers receive, we still need to manage the time spent on paperwork. Try to handle each paper as few times as possible; once is often enough. Scan the paper. Recycle it immediately if there is no reason to keep it. As with other "incoming" interruptions, you can set aside a certain time to address the papers that come across your desks. If some action is needed and it's appropriate to do so, do it now. Often interoffice memos can be answered by writing the reply on the bottom of the page, saving the time needed for a formal response.

As you read correspondence that requires action, note on the letter or an attached paper what must be done, such as obtain additional information, write a response, etc. If this is done at the time you read the letter, it will obviate the need to reread the letter when you are ready to take that action.

When reading reports, read the summary first. Often there is no need to read the entire report. You can then choose to read whatever other information is necessary and save the time of reading details that are of little value to you.

Unnecessary Red Tape

An inordinate amount of time is spent in many organizations on filling out forms, duplicating documents, and other forms of unnecessary red tape and recordkeeping.

As Robinson Wyler, vice president of branch operations of a major California bank, was walking through one of his bank's offices, he noticed that one of the clerks was busily engaged in filling out a pink form. "Aren't you aware," he asked her, "that the information on this pink form is now in the computer and the pink form is no longer needed?" She looked puzzled. "Of course I know this data is in the computer," she responded. "I do the data input, but nobody ever told me that I should discontinue using the pink form."

Further investigation brought out that although, the information had been computerized over a year earlier, nobody had issued a directive to discontinue the pink form. Many firms continue to use forms that have outlived their usefulness —at great expense in time, money and effort—because nobody took the necessary steps to discontinue them.

Every standardized report, form letter, or other printed document that is repeatedly used should be tried for its life periodically. When should this evaluation take place? At the minimum, no form or document should be used for more than two years without being given careful reevaluation to determine its value. If any significant change is made in the area in which the form is used, such as the introduction of new methods or equipment, this evaluation should be accomplished as soon as the new methods or equipment have been in place long enough to determine how they affect the total operation. Another good time to study the value of a form or similar document when it is time to reorder it. If this had been done at the California bank at the time the pink forms were scheduled for reprinting, their obsolescence would have been noted.

Form letters should be reevaluated in the same manner as reports and other documents. If the form letter sounds too impersonal or does not clearly answer the question it has been designed to handle, it should be rewritten. Remember, the image of your organization is projected to the reader by that letter.

If all forms, systems, reports, and standardized letters are critically assessed periodically, not only will countless hours of unneeded work be eliminated, but employees will be able to devote more of their time and energy to the matters that are really important to reaching the goals which you and your organization desire to reach.

> *Until we can manage our time, we can manage nothing else.*
>
> Peter F Drucker

Expect the Unexpected

In every job, unexpected things develop during the day. Fires have to be put out, machines or computers break down, the boss has a special project, an employee gives you a problem. You expect these events to occur, but you never know just what they will be or when they will happen.

To avoid permitting these time robbers to completely disrupt your schedules, build into the time plan a certain amount of leeway to handle the unexpected. By analyzing your day's activities over a period of time, you can determine just how many hours each day are spent dealing with the unexpected. If, for example, in a typical eight-hour day, two hours are used up by these emergencies, then plan only for a six-hour day. In that way, the unexpected becomes expected, and you have the time to manage it.

It is unlikely that anybody can plan a day and have it go exactly as intended. The time robbers will always be there, ready to destroy your well planned day. But by being aware of these time robbers, you can minimize the losses of the valuable minutes and come closer to making the most of your time.

Change Provides Opportunities

When stress gets you down, restore calm in your life by filling your mind with thoughts of peace, courage, health and hope. Being calm will get you through the situation that stresses you. If you continue to hold our head high and present a public face of peacefulness, your friends and coworkers will respect you and help you with your concerns.

And as noted earlier in this chapter, stress is not always a negative experience. Times of change may be stress-inducing, but they may also be defining moments in our lives. They give us the opportunity to reassess our job and our career. Changes may encourage us to take steps to rethink our goals and move toward fulfilling them.

Sum and Substance

- Most of us feel added stress when changes are being made in some aspect of our jobs.
- It is possible to cope with most stressful situations by applying one or more of the stress-reducers listed in the acronym, "STRESS."

  S elf-Awareness.

  T ender Loving Care. Taking care of oneself is important to good health and people in good health are less likely to be stressed.

  R elaxation.

  E xercise.

  S ense of Humor.

  S eek help from others. Sometimes stress is so overwhelming one cannot cope alone. Professional counselors, clergy, and specialists in specific areas can be called upon to help.

- Instead of worrying that you will have problems with the changes that are being instituted, deal with each concern and take steps to overcome it.
- To solve your problems, follow Dale Carnegie's formula:

  Get all the facts.

  Weigh all the facts, and then come to a decision.

  Once a decision is reached, act!
- When people are asked what causes them to be stressed, one of the most frequent responses is "There isn't enough time to do what must be done." Carefully managing one's time can minimize this problem.
- When stress gets you down, restore calm in your lives by filling your mind with thoughts of peace, courage, health and hope.
- Make a point of seeing changes as opportunities.

7

DEALING WITH DIVERSE PEOPLE

Good leadership requires us to surround ourselves with people of diverse perspectives who can disagree with us without fear of retaliation.

Doris Kearns Goodwin

The world of the twenty-first century is a more complex, diverse environment than in years past. Your coworkers, subordinates, managers, and customers may look, speak, behave and think differently than you do. Rather than expect these people to be like you, you need to recognize and respect the unique perspectives and qualities of individuals. Your success in your jobs today requires that you have a greater sense of awareness about all people and demonstrate agility in relating to them.

It is important to understand the differences among the men and women with whom you work and how these differences affect the nature of your interrelationship. You must develop strategies that allow you to approach people in ways that are effective and productive for them and focus on finding ways to drive greater personal and team success.

In this chapter we will discuss dealing with the following areas:

- Making the most of the ethnic and cultural backgrounds of your associates.
- Communicating with people who have difficulty understanding or speaking your language.
- The special problems of working with people with physical or mental disabilities.

In the following chapter we will concentrate on:

- Working with people in age groups different from yours.
- Dealing with problems relating to gender differences in the workplace.

> *One of the major contributions of behavioral science to management is that all people are individuals and they differ from one another. To work effectively with people, get to know them and tailor our way of dealing with them to their individualities.*
>
> Arthur R Pell, Ph.D.

Understanding Cultural Differences

Culture may be broadly described as what defines each of us on the basis of geography, language, customs and beliefs. The people and institutions within your own culture play a major role in how you see the world and those around you. Depending upon how strong those past experiences and influences have been, they may affect the ways in which you respond to individuals you encounter who you perceive to be outside of your own culture.

Glossary of Terms

Much has been written about working with diverse groups and in many countries laws have been enacted on relations with diverse groups in the workplace. To better understand this, it is helpful to understand the terminology commonly used. Here are some of these words:

Acceptance: Experience of a situation or condition without an attempt to change it.

Ageism: Negative attitudes, beliefs or practices toward a group based upon age.

Assimilation: Voluntary/involuntary acceptance by minority groups of some aspects of the dominant group.

Assumption: Taken for granted; believed to be true without proof that the culture, religion or other characteristic of one group is superior to that of others.

Bias: Personal inclination of temperament or outlook. Prejudice for or against members of one or more types of people.

Bigotry: Intolerance for the beliefs or practices of others.

Discrimination: Unfair treatment of an individual or group based upon a prejudice.

Ethnocentrism: Belief that members of one's own ethnic group are superior to members of other groups.

Generalization: Sweeping statement presented as a general truth.

Intolerance: Unwillingness or refusal to accept differences.

Prejudice: Negative attitude often formed without knowledge or basis.

Racism: Negative beliefs about a group of people based upon race, unfair treatment of an individual or group based upon race.

Segregation: Separation or isolation of an individual or group.

Sexism: Attitudes and behaviors based upon stereotypical gender roles.

Stereotype: Broadly attributing characteristics to all members of a group despite individual differences.

Tolerance: Capacity to recognize and respect the beliefs and practices of others.

> *Of all the various delusions, the sense of discrimination between oneself and others is the worst form, as it creates nothing but unpleasantness.*
>
> The Dalai Lama

Assessment: Values Awareness

In order to better understand one's attitude regarding the cultural differences between oneself and of others, write, "agree" or "disagree" next to the following statements:

1. As a child, I was raised to celebrate specific holidays related to my country of origin or religious beliefs.
2. As an adult, I am proud of the culture in which I grew up and the clear rules of behavior I learned.
3. My religion requires me to observe specific traditions as an act of faith.

4. By choice, there are additional observances each year that are important to me based upon my interests, religion, gender, age or other factors.
5. Most of my associates know little or nothing about my background and values.
6. I believe that religious and cultural observances should be a private matter.
7. I am familiar with the cultural backgrounds and religious beliefs of my coworkers.
8. I respect and celebrate the cultural observances and traditions of those on my team.
9. I openly share the significance of my own cultural celebrations.
10. Only the official holidays of this country should be honored at work.
11. I find some of the customs, traditions and/or observances of my colleagues to be curious or offensive.
12. Our workplace would be more harmonious if all of us shared the same values.

Understanding is the first step to acceptance.

J K Rowling

Evaluation of Responses

If the response was "agree" to items 1–4:

This may indicate a strong connection to your own cultural and religious traditions and values. On the one hand, this connection may provide you with a strong sense of purpose, offer guidance for ethical behavior and be a comfort in unfamiliar or stressful situations. On the other hand, your personal experiences and strong beliefs may make it harder for you to accept or tolerate views that differ from the ones we hold.

If the response was "agree" to items 5–6:

This may indicate that you are reserved about openly expressing your own values and believe that others should behave likewise. On a positive note, this approach may avoid conflict and confrontation when differences do exist. At the same time, a lack of awareness could actually cause problems based upon insensitive comments or behaviors to which others may take exception.

If the response was "agree" to items 7–9:

These answers may be interpreted as demonstrating openness to others and viewing differences as being interesting rather than irritating. A benefit of these attitudes is that they can lead to building rapport with colleagues. A downside may be that others could see you as less than strong in your own convictions.

If the response was "agree" to items 10–12:

By agreeing with these statements, you may be viewed as being a purist in terms of cultural values and more. An advantage of holding these ideas may include fostering a homogeneous workplace when willingly embraced by all. A possible disadvantage is that such attitudes can easily alienate members of the group who hold differences of opinions and practice other styles.

As we become ever more diverse, we must work harder to unite around our common values and our common humanity.

William Jefferson Clinton

Know and Overcome Your Biases

People often make decisions based on factors they may not even realize are biases.

After the Achilles Heel Company rejected Pierre W for a sales job, he was hired by a direct competitor and became the best salesperson on their staff. When Achilles' sales manager was asked why he had rejected Pierre, he said: "I guess it was because he had a foreign accent."

How many good people have you rejected because of your conscious or subconscious biases?

The word "bias" means "slant." In hiring or dealing with people on the job, we tend to slant toward people who fit our preconceived notions of what will or will not make for success in that job. Often these preconceptions are wrong—based on concepts that do not necessarily hold up when carefully examined. The word "prejudice" means "prejudgment." The decision is made on the basis of some superficial characteristic before a real evaluation of qualifications is conducted.

Sometimes, we reject people because of a specific personal characteristic that annoys us. Remember that what bothers one person, such as Pierre's accent, is not necessarily going to bother others and in fact may be attractive to them.

People Like Ourselves

Our biases are based not only on how a person speaks, looks, or dresses, but other aspects of his or her background also play an important role. People tend to feel more comfortable with people like themselves. We tend to be biased in favor of people who have similar backgrounds, who attended the same school or even live in the same community.

The president of a bank was of Serbian descent. By strange coincidence, most of the people he personally hired or promoted had Serbian backgrounds. Occasionally, an unusually competent person from another background might be promoted to a management job—but never a Croatian. Why? From childhood he had been inculcated with the rivalry between these two Slavic cultures.

On the surface, this action may appear to be sensible. After all, people who work together must be compatible. But not only was this illegal—discrimination based on national origin—but allowing a person's nationality to be a major hurdle in his or her career may eliminate high-potential people who could have been significant contributors to the company's success.

It's Not Bias—It's Fact

Jack was annoyed. "I am not biased," he explained when criticized for his choice of salespeople. "You have to be good-looking to be successful in sales. People do judge a book by its cover. Buyers are more likely to spend time with an impressive-looking person. They turn the plain ones away."

However, when Jack was asked to compare his salespeople's results with those of other managers who did not put as much emphasis on looks when hiring, he realized that his "fact" was not true. The best salesperson in the company was a man Jack had refused to hire in his territory because he walked with a cane. "Customers would be turned off by a cripple," he explained. His boss pointed out that often people with physical disadvantages compensate for it by working harder and smarter than their so-called "normal" competitors.

Uncovering Our Own Biases

Most people accept the fact that we should evaluate someone be based on his or her whole background. Because many biases are subconscious, however, many of us do not realize what our biases are. Biases are emotional, not logical. Only by careful self-analysis can we become aware of them.

To do this, review the job openings you have filled—either by hiring or promotion—over the past year. Look at the people you have chosen. Do they have any one special characteristic in common? Do they have the same type of appearance, speech, or ethnic background as one another?

Give special attention to the rejected applicants, particularly those who never proceeded beyond the first interview or consideration. Were they really unqualified? Did they have something about them that we could not define, but just didn't like? If so, it could have been good personnel intuition—or be honest—were your biases showing?

Making the Most of Diversity

Once you become aware of and take steps to overcome your biases, you should examine the entire concept of working with diverse people in your organization. If you are in management, you should make successful diversity practices a primary mission. If you are in nonmanagerial job, you should work with your managers and coworkers to achieve a successful relationship with people different from you.

The first phase of making the most of diversity is to make a concerted effort to become aware of the cultural diversity that exists within our organization.

The second phase of making the most of diversity is for people to talk about their cultural differences. Two things must be remembered concerning cultural diversity:

- People should remember it is difficult to address cultural differences without resorting to stereotypes. In the purest form, there is no such thing as a stereotypical person. No person is exactly like another person and no individual is a clone of another member of a group.
- As diversity in an organization grows, so does the complexity of communication and the necessity to make greater efforts in developing improved communication skills.

Awareness and discussion can cause a clearer picture of cultural diversity. Appreciation and understanding of cultural diversity is more than just tolerating differences among individuals or groups, but supporting and nurturing them. A variety of ideas, talents, skills and knowledge are desirable attributes of any organization.

Providing a supportive and nurturing environment and exposing group members to new issues, ideas, information and cultures, enhances other goals of the organization. Openly addressing diversity creates opportunities for character development by teaching tolerance and respect for people and by encouraging concern for equity. A culturally diverse coalition that values and nurtures people from all backgrounds is worthy of active participation. Such an organization will flourish and perpetuate.

Making the most of diversity requires the commitment of all involved. Changing prevailing attitudes and assumptions is not easy. Often the best we can hope for is to change behaviors rather than deep-seated attitudes. Members of a diverse coalition must be committed to multiculturalism and to addressing issues related to cultural difference.

Enhancing the Dynamics of Multiculturism

People in most countries today face the problems inherent in working with diverse groups. From the middle of the twentieth century, companies in Europe and Asia have "imported" workers from less developed countries to work in their workplaces. We have seen mass emigrations of Turks to Germany, Algerians to France, Indonesians and South Asians to Saudi Arabia, Koreans to Japan and many others.

Early in our history, the American experience differed from that in other countries because the early immigrants relatively rapidly assimilated into the American lifestyle. This is not what has happened in recent times.

Under the traditional melting-pot theory, immigrants who settled in America would shed the ways of the old countries and blend happily into one people. This type of assimilation has been replaced by the multicultural concept. More recent immigrants tend to hang on to their native cultures and integrate them with the culture of their new environment without abandoning them.

Since the 1960s, the idea of a single monoculture has begun to deteriorate. It has given way to a more pluralistic society that continues to evolve through cultural integration and influence. These changes are commonly evident in fashion, dietary habits, entertainment, music, literature and sports.

Such diversity enables all of us to capitalize on unique skills and areas of expertise. We can learn much by mutual understanding and appreciation of individual differences. Strengthening people's sense of positive cultural identity is an important aspect of establishing a successful relationship among all involved. Individuals may consciously or subconsciously interject ethnic values, attitudes or behaviors into the dynamics of the larger group.

Managing Cultural Diversity

To make the most of cultural diversity, programs and protocols should include:

1. *Recruitment.*

   Try to include people in your organization that are representative of the community.

2. *Diversity Training.*

   Become aware of the cultural diversity of the group. Try to understand all its dimensions and seek the commitment of those involved to nurture cultural diversity. Address the myths, stereotypes and cultural differences that interfere with the full contribution of members.

3. *Communications Within Coalitions.*

   Remove the major barriers that interfere with people from diverse cultures working together. The best method to do this is through understanding and practicing better communication:

   - Learn to listen. Listen for what is really being said, not what we want to hear.

- Invite others to be a part of the discussion.
- Learn to communicate clearly and fairly.
- Do not misjudge people because of their accent or grammar.
- Test for understanding. Ask questions to be certain you are clear on what is being said.
- Adapt your communication style to fit the situation. Be explicit. Individuals from different cultures may react differently to certain language and tone. Know with whom you are communicating.
- Use language that fosters trust and alliance. Each person wants to succeed in this venture. Be calm and positive.
- When conflicts arise, the problem may result from style rather than content. Strive for understanding. Review, revise, and revisit your main objective to be certain the content is clear. How you say something may be more important than what you say.

4. *Different, But the Same.*

   Men and women, whites and people of color, managers and workers are different from one another, but their similarities outweigh such differences. An appreciation and acceptance of both commonalities and differences are essential to effective working relationships.

5. *Maintain the Commitment.*

   Your organization will become more connected with the community that it serves if it states publicly that having a diverse work force is a top priority. Continue to revisit the various activities that ensure the awareness, understanding, communication, and nurturing of a culturally diverse organization.

6. *Provide Strong Leadership.*
    - Articulate pluralistic vision and values for the organization; show ways in which they are an integral part of the organization's mission and vision.
    - Encourage and support discussion among people throughout the organization about the meaning of diversity and pluralism; show how to implement programs that can accomplish those goals.
    - Demonstrate ethical commitment to fairness and to the elimination of discrimination in all its forms inside the organization and in its relationships to other people, groups, and organizations.
    - Understand the dimensions of diversity, use inclusive and valuing language, quote diverse sources, readily adapt to differences in communication styles of diverse people, display respect for human differences and be aware of and comfortable about dealing with diversity issues.
    - Value ongoing personal learning and change, solicit views and opinions of diverse people, invite feedback about personal behavior and blind spots and be open to belief modifications and actions based on feedback.
    - Mentor and empower diverse individuals and encourage others to do so as well.

Working with People with Language Deficiencies

When working with people who have limited knowledge of your language, supervisors and associates must make special efforts to assure that they understand what you say to them and you understand what they say to you.

If your organization employs a large number of immigrants or guest workers from the same country, it may be advisable to hire one or more bilingual interpreters. However, this is not always feasible. Most workers learn enough of our language for basic communication. Usually there are other employees from their country to assist in clarifying communication.

When working with nonnative speakers, and particularly with those who barely speak the language at all, it helps to have materials translated into the appropriate languages so these employees can learn the job as well as a native speaker.

Multilingual materials.

Bilingual or multilingual tools like booklets, quickreference cards, employee manuals and menus are helpful when training someone new. Simple work-related rules, such as instructions for clocking in and clocking out in each of the languages frequently spoken in the organization, may be provided.

Some organizations provide audiotapes or videotapes to employees to help bridge the language gap. The tapes include important words and phrases to help nonnative speakers with the terminology of the organization.

On occasion, a company will offer education as part of the benefit package. This allows employees the means to study your language as a second language on a deeper level, improving confidence and skills in the job and the community.

Visual tools can include posters that outline the proper step-by-step procedures for performing manual jobs.

Making Sure You are Understood

Speak clearly and pronounce your words correctly.

Exaggerated pronunciations will not help the listener and

may cause more confusion. However, it may be helpful to pronounce some words as the nonnative speaker does. This will be especially true if the proper pronunciation is very different from the nonnative pronunciation.

Speaking more loudly is not helpful.

Recognize that people wrongly think that turning up the volume somehow creates instant understanding. Avoid this common mistake (however, do not speak too quietly).

Do not cover or hide our mouth.

Listeners will want to watch us as you pronounce your words. Being able to see someone enunciate can be helpful in understanding what is being said.

Avoid running words together.

One of the biggest challenges for a listener is knowing where one word ends and the next one begins. A small pause between words can be useful if your listener seems to be struggling.

When possible, opt for simple words instead of ones that are complex.

The more basic a word is, the better the chance is that it will be understood. For example, in the English language, use "big" rather than "enormous." "Make" is a better choice than "manufacture." However, with a Romance-language speaker (i.e., Spanish, French, Italian, Portuguese, Romanian), often more complex words can be useful as they are rooted in Latin.

Avoid using "filler" words and colloquialisms.

Nonnative speakers, especially those of lower proficiency levels, may get hung up on "filler" sounds and informal expressions. They may think that filler sounds such as "er" or "um" are vocabulary words that they don't possess. Colloquialisms such as "It's raining cats are dogs," are likely to be unknown as well and can easily be misunderstood. Also, avoid using contractions or short forms.

If asked to repeat something, first repeat it as said the first time.

It's best to use the same wording when we're asked to repeat ourselves; it could be that we were just not heard clearly. If the listener still doesn't understand, however, change a few key words in the sentence. It may be that only one or two of the words were not understood. Also, it is best to repeat the whole sentence and not just the last couple of words. This practice is time consuming, but it helps prevent confusion.

Paraphrase.

If there is a similar word to the word that is not understood, use it. As knowledge of our listeners' comprehension of our language grows, communicating becomes even easier.

Be explicit.

Say "yes" or "no." Do not say: "uh-huh" or "uh-uh." Those words are not in grammar books!

Listen and try not to form your response while the other person is talking.

Wait until the person is done so that we can clarify if needed and give correct information based on all they have said.

Be aware that other cultures have different standards regarding touching, eye contact and personal space.

Someone standing too closely or not looking us in the eye is merely following his or her own cultural standard and not trying to offend. Avoid touching listeners from some cultures. Even if you want to nudge them in the right direction or encourage them with a friendly pat on the back our gesture may be misinterpreted. People of many cultures view personal contact very differently from the way we tend to as Americans, and your friendly touch could be seen as aggressive or overly familiar.

Be patient and smile.

The more relaxed we are, the greater our control over communication. Do not give a busy lifestyle or a meeting agenda permission to control our speech. Think as we speak and do not speak as we think.

> *Our greatest strength as a human race is our ability to acknowledge our differences. Our greatest weakness is our failure to embrace them.*
>
> Judith Henderson

Quick Tips for Working with People of Different Cultures

- Most people appreciate a sincere effort to reach out, be greeted in their own language and to have their beliefs acknowledged. Don't worry about making mistakes.
- It may take longer to build rapport and trust with people from different cultures. Be patient.
- Ask people involved to let you know at any time if you do something that is offensive in their culture.
- Thoroughly explain the procedures that you propose to conduct and the reason for doing them.

- In communicating with people who have limited proficiency in your language:
    1. if the material is technical or complex, use a trained interpreter,
    2. for simpler matters, get help from another associate who has a good knowledge of both languages involved.
- As much as possible, use words (not gestures) to express your meaning. Gestures that are acceptable in your culture may be offensive or meaningless in other cultures.
- Find out how the person views the matter being discussed. The following questions may be used as a guide:
    1. How do you see this situation?
    2. What do you think caused it?
    3. How does it affect your work?
    4. What have you done so far to deal with it?
    5. What kind of help can we provide?

Disabled Members of the Workforce

> *Not only do physically disabled people have experiences which are not available to the able-bodied, they are in a better position to transcend cultural mythologies about the body, because they cannot do things the able-bodied feel they must do in order to be happy, "normal," and sane. If disabled people were truly heard, an explosion of knowledge of the human body and psyche would take place.*
>
> Susan Wendell

Staff members at many companies throughout the world realize that people with disabilities are productive, reliable employees who bring benefits to the workplace. Some companies also engage in developing products and services for people with disabilities, their families, and friends. And, as companies engage with communities in which they do business, many pay specific attention to disabled persons.

These themes are the basis of *Disability in the Workplace: Company Practices*, a publication of the International Labor Organization, a United Nations affiliate. The report describes the contemporary experiences of twenty five companies and their work on the issue of disability. The profiles describe company practices toward disabled persons as employees or potential employees, customers and consumers and community members. The descriptions are short, only two to four pages, but each capture the context of company operations as it relates to the issue of disability.

This report is timely for many reasons. It comes in the wake of a major global economic crisis, yet the companies profiled have nevertheless given strength to their disability and diversity initiatives. It provides inspiration and guidance to companies at a time when countries are ratifying and seeking to implement the U.N. Convention on the Rights of Persons with Disabilities, a comprehensive human rights convention for people with disabilities that will require some changes in national policies and practices related to work and employment. *Disability in the Workplace: Company Practices* also responds to an emerging body of information that supports the business case for hiring people with disabilities and the interest of companies to maintain diverse workforces.

Companies hire people with disabilities and address their needs in products and services for many reasons. People with disabilities make good, dependable employees. Many cases document comparable productivity, lower accident rates and higher job retention rates between employees with disabilities and a company's general workforce.

People with disabilities represent an often untapped source of skill and talent, including technical skills if they have access to training, and transferable problem-solving skills developed in daily life. People who develop disabilities while working often have valuable skills and experiences learned on the job, in addition to their formal skills qualifications.

Hiring people with disabilities can contribute to the overall diversity, creativity, and morale of the workplace, as well as, enhance a company's image among its staff, in the community and among customers. A concern for human rights and nondiscriminatory practices are also reflected in the company profiles. Many illustrate International Labor Organization (ILO) principles, including those articulated in the *ILO Code of Practice on Managing Disability in the Workplace* and in ILO standards. These businesses provide inspiration and guidance for companies in advancing their nondiscrimination and diversity policies and initiatives. Among many measures, the convention calls for nondiscrimination and reasonable accommodation to promote access to training and employment.

A study of the practices related to the companies' internal operation include:

- Policy statements related to nondiscrimination and inclusion of disabled persons.
- Measures to make the workplace, printed materials, the

online environment and commercial outlets or distribution points accessible.

- Employee disability networks (see "affinity groups" below).
- Disability awareness training for management and coworkers.
- Practices to promote the training, hiring or retention of disabled persons and to enhance their productivity.
- Specific recruitment or community outreach techniques and programs.
- Internships, training programs and mentoring or leadership programs specifically oriented to those with disabilities.
- Reasonable accommodation to meet individual needs.
- Allocation of designated human-resource or management staff trained or knowledgeable about work-related disability issues.
- Policies and practices for business-to-business relationships with entrepreneurs with disabilities. Employee volunteer programs.
- Collaboration with unions, nongovernmental organizations and governments.
- Collaboration with disabled persons' organizations, including with regard to disability awareness training, accessibility and product development.
- Adherence to accessibility standards, both online and in the physical environment and active promotion of such standards.

Participation in business groups and networks related to disability issues.

Disability is a matter of perception. If you can do just one thing well, you're needed by someone.

Martina Navratilova

Disabled Employees On the Job

Several countries, including the United States, Canada, the United Kingdom, Germany, France and Japan, have passed laws prohibiting discrimination against disabled people in the workplace. There are many facets to these laws. The main aspect for all employees to know is that it is now illegal to discriminate in the hiring, job assignment and treatment of employees because of a disability. Employers must make reasonable accommodations so disabled people can perform the essential duties of the job.

Such accommodations might include building ramps for wheelchairs, providing special equipment for the seeing-and hearing-impaired, making other physical changes in the facilities and minor adjustments in work schedules or systems.

Let's look at a specific situation. Cara is a highly qualified accountant but because she uses a wheelchair, she cannot get to the second floor of the building where the accounting department is located. As it is not possible to build a ramp in this two-story building, a simple accommodation would be to allow Cara to work on the first floor and have her work brought to her. An inconvenience, yes—but it is a reasonable accommodation.

When evaluating handicapped applicants for employment, you should concentrate on the applicant's capabilities, not disabilities. Often what appears to be an obstacle to successful performance is only a perception, which can be overcome with reasonable accommodation.

The Hiring Process

Dorothy, a highly skilled word processor operator, was legally blind. She could transcribe from dictated material faster and more accurately than many sighted people. She walked with the aid of a white cane and after being led to a specific place once or twice, could get there and back easily without help. Although the human resources staff highly recommended her employment, Beth, the word processing-department supervisor, did not want to hire her. "I'm afraid," she said, "that in case of a fire or other emergency, she would be a danger to herself and others in the department."

Beth's concern was reasonable; we cannot overlook problems that may occur, even though their likelihood is slight. In this case, by assigning somebody to escort Dorothy in the event of an emergency, the concern was alleviated.

Working Conditions

Ted was badly injured in an automobile accident. His job in the factory required that he stand at a workbench all day. When he was ready to return to work, he was unable to stand for such a long period. His supervisor, Russ, sent Ted home and told him that until he could do the job, he could not work.

What Russ should have done was to determine if some accommodation could be made. Perhaps a high stool could have been provided so Ted could reach the workbench without having to stand. If this were not feasible, Ted's hours could have been adjusted so he could work part-time on that job and do other work that did not require standing for the balance of the day.

Attitude of Other Employees

It is not only managers and supervisors who must assure fair opportunities are provided to people with disabilities. It applies to all employees. Some workers may resent having to give special treatment to a disabled person, especially, if it increases his or her workload or involves some inconvenience.

The mechanics in the Tool Manufacturing Co. spent about 80 percent of their work time in the shop fixing and adjusting various pieces of equipment. About 20 percent of their work required going out to the factory floor installing, fixing or adjusting heavy equipment that could not be brought into the shop. As this work was more strenuous and often physically uncomfortable, the mechanics referred to it as "dirty work" and they took turns when such assignments came up.

Chad, the newly hired mechanic, was a whiz at fixing things, had "magic hands" and the type of mental acuity that could identify mechanical problems rapidly and come up with imaginative solutions. But Chad was unable to walk without the aid of two canes. It was no problem to get to the shop, but when the job required going to a machine in other places in the plant, he could not maneuver through the plant to the equipment and was unable to go through the physical contortions necessary to reach inside and around this machinery.

To accommodate for this disability, Tom, the master mechanic, arranged for all of Chad's work to be done in the shop. The other mechanics would handle the outside work. After a while, the amount of time each of the other mechanics had to give to the "dirty work" increased and they began to resent it. "Why should we have to spend so much time on these tough jobs and he gets away with the light stuff?" they complained. "They should hire a guy who can do it all."

When Tom heard these gripes, he was perplexed. He did not want to fire Chad. Not only was he a good mechanic, but also it would violate the law. Yet, the morale in the department was falling and it was reflected in productivity and in the manner the others were treating Chad. Tom felt this could best be handled by one-to-one discussions with each of his mechanics. He decided to follow some proven principles of dealing with people. He told each of them how much he appreciated the good work they had been doing and he asked them whether they agreed that Chad was also a good mechanic. Of course, they had to agree; he was good. He asked them to look at Chad's position. He was contributing a good deal to the department. Many of his ideas had helped each of them solve problems they had faced. The only disadvantage to having Chad on the team was his inability to do the "dirty work." "What did this mean to them?" Tom asked. He referred to the job sheets and showed them that the added time each had given to these in-shop assignments was only a few hours more each week. Then he appealed to their nobler motives. "You all like Chad. He has proven to be a valuable asset to this department. You're not going to let a few extra hours a week of 'dirty work' prevent Chad from utilizing his talents to make a living?"

After these talks, things turned around. The mechanics all went out of their way to let Chad know they liked and appreciated him. By taking the initiative in handling the disturbance, Tom restored morale and productivity and helped his company meet both the letter and the spirit of the law.

Other Techniques to Assist the Disabled at Work

Some additional steps companies may take to help disabled employees on the job are:

- Create a resource group for employees with disabilities.
- Offer dependent-care benefits (including childcare and eldercare).
- Provide stories or videos of people with disabilities on corporate websites.
- Provide mandatory diversity training for all employees.

Affinity Groups for Employees with Disabilities

Some organizations have gone much farther in their efforts to make workers in minority groups more comfortable in the work environment. They created niche groups of such employees, generally called "affinity groups."

Women and minority employees in many companies in the United States have had considerable success utilizing their affinity groups to climb the corporate ladder. Employees with disabilities can similarly benefit in terms of professional growth and leadership development, ultimately resulting in promotion opportunities.

Dr Robert S. Rudney, Senior Advisor Studies & Analyses at the United States Air Force, made a study of affinity groups for disabled employees in major U.S. companies. Some of his findings follow.

Employees with disabilities are increasingly recognizing the value of forming affinity groups to represent their interests with their employer and to promote disability education and outreach within the organization's culture. For their part, employers are welcoming the creation of disability affinity groups as part of their diversity commitment and also as marketing mechanisms for improving products and services to customers with disabilities.

The affinity group connection can be vital in the on-boarding process for new employees with disabilities. Even with their accommodations in place, these employees may need assistance and advice in navigating buildings and websites and understanding corporate policies and procedures. Experienced members of affinity groups often establish formal or informal mentoring relationships with new hires. Perhaps more importantly in today's economic climate, disability affinity groups can provide their members with job-retention strategies and internal networking contacts for those seeking to transition internally because of impending layoffs.

Employers can also utilize affinity group networks to explain policy changes or to request feedback on policy initiatives under consideration. Affinity groups have advised employers on accommodation policies and implementation, as well as, sensitivity and awareness training. Externally, a disability affinity group can operate as an effective recruitment tool to bring qualified job applicants with disabilities into the organization. Networking is the way 60 percent of jobs are found, but, for mobility, communications or simple self-confidence reasons, people with disabilities often have a hard time networking. At the same time, disability employment groups and rehabilitation providers need to do a better job of identifying and linking up with internal affinity groups at an employer site.

Members of the affinity group can reflect the preferences of the disabled customer base regarding the company's products and services. The disability employee's affinity group at Best

Buy, a major U.S. retailer of home appliance and electronic equipment, was instrumental in convincing the company to provide an in-store closed-captioning option for its home-theater promotions to appeal to prospective customers with hearing impairments.

Hewlett Packard's Employee Resource Group has contributed significantly to the usability of new products and the incorporation of universal design features. Ford Employees Disability group reviews new car designs for accessibility. As a consequence, both Hewlett Packard and Ford—like many other employers—have realized a return on investment by supporting an affinity group for its employees with disabilities.

The National Affinity Leadership Congress has developed additional information about affinity groups for the disabled.

(See *www.nalc.diversitybestpractices.com* for more information on the organization's offerings.)

Sum and Substance

- The people and institutions within our own culture play a major role in how we see the world and those around us. They may affect the ways in which we respond to individuals we encounter who we perceive to be outside of our own culture.
- Because many biases are subconscious, many of us do not realize what our biases are. Biases are emotional not logical. Only by careful self-analysis can we become aware of them.
- Once you become aware of and take steps to overcome your biases, you should examine the entire concept of working with diverse people in your organization. If you are in management, you should make this a primary mission.

If you are in nonmanagerial jobs, you should work with your managers and coworkers to achieve a successful relationship with people different from you.

- Appreciation and understanding of cultural diversity is more than just tolerating differences among individuals or groups, but supporting and nurturing them.
- When working with people who have limited knowledge of your language, you must make special efforts to ensure that they understand what you say to them and you understand what they say to you.
- Diversity enables all of us to capitalize on unique skills and areas of expertise. You can learn much by mutual understanding and appreciation of individual differences. Strengthening the positive attributes of cultural identity is an important aspect of establishing a successful relationship among all involved.
- Developing a deeper understanding of your coworkers enhances your ability to create and maintain an environment that fosters mutual respect and cooperation.
- When considering a person with a disability for employment, focus on his or her abilities, not his or her disabilities.
- People with disabilities represent a widely untapped source of skills and talent, including technical skills if they have access to training, and transferable problem-solving skills developed in daily life. In addition, people who develop disabilities while working often have valuable skills and experiences learned on the job, in addition to their formal skills and qualifications.
- By making reasonable accommodations, people with disabilities can become valuable, productive workers.

8

DIVERSITY IN GENDER AND AGE

In the previous chapter, we discussed dealing with people in our workplace who come from different cultures and with the disabled. In this chapter we will look at the special issues that arise when dealing with gender differences and with people of different age groups.

Gender Relations

Dealing unfairly with a person at work due to his or her gender is discrimination. In this book, we are primarily concerned with the actions of all individuals in the workplace, and so our focus will be on the treatment of our coworkers, subordinates, and others with whom we interrelate. Management-based discrimination may take the form of failure to hire or to promote a person, or the determination of someone's salary or wages based on that person's gender. As the above actions are those only of a business's leadership, we will not discuss these facets of the subject.

Changes in Reporting Relations

Sexual Harassment

Sexual harassment is one form of workplace discrimination that need not be related to the management-staff member relationship. Sexual harassment involves intimidation, bullying or coercion of a sexual nature or the unwelcome or inappropriate promise of rewards in exchange for sexual favors. It includes a range of behavior from what might be perceived as relatively inocuous transgressions and annoyances to physical or emotional abuse. For many businesses and other organizations, preventing sexual harassment and defending employees from sexual harassment charges have become significant human resources responsibilities.

Common professional, academic, financial and social effects of sexual harassment include:

- Diminished work performance.
- Increased absenteeism.
- Invaded privacy of one's personal life.
- Being objectified and humiliated by scrutiny and gossip.
- Defamation of character and reputation.
- Loss of trust in environments similar to where the harassment occurred.
- Loss of trust in supervisors or management.
- Extreme stress upon the personal life of the harassed person.
- Physical or mental health problems caused by the harassment.
- Loss of references/recommendations.
- Loss of job or career, loss of income

Legislation designed to protect workers from sexual harassment in the workplace exists in many countries including the United States, Canada, the United Kingdom, members of the European Union, Japan, and India. Under these laws employers are required to protect employees from ill-treatment based on their gender, and they're required to take all possible preventive measures against sexual harassment. In addition, employers are financially liable for cases of misconduct.

Sex Harassment is a Costly Offense

To avoid sexual harassment problems caused by one or more of their employees, companies must make overt efforts to assure that all employees—not just management—are aware of and in compliance with apprpriate laws and policies. Failure to do so can cost the company a lot of money. For example, in 1998, the Mitsubishi Company settled a sexual harassment suit by agreeing to pay $34 million to 360 women who had been harassed in its plant in Normal, Illinois.

The women reported that they had been fondled by male workers, propositioned by supervisors, called crude, sexually explicit names, subjected to viewing pornographic graffiti on the walls and generally mistreated. Management ignored their complaints.

In Long Island, New York, several women employees of Smith Barney, one of the top stock brokerage firms, accused their managers of creating a hostile and offensive working environment. They reported that the employee lounge was nicknamed the "boom-boom" room and that male employees made passes at the women there and considered it "good fun" to make sexually oriented remarks.

Women in other Smith Barney offices joined the class action. A federal court ordered the firm to submit the claims to an arbitration board to determine how much each individual claimant should be paid. In addition, the company was ordered to institute a diversity training program to recruit, train and promote women to jobs within the company where they were underrepresented. The total cost was estimated to be over $15 million.

The courts in several countries have ruled that a company can be forced to pay damages to its workers who are sexually harassed by a low-level supervisor, even if they company knew nothing of the harassment and the victim failed to complain.

What Exactly Is Sexual Harassment?

While demanding sexual favors for favorable treatment on the job is an obvious form of sexual harassment, the legal definition of sexual harassment covers a broader range of activities.

Any unwelcome sexual advance or request for sexual favors or any conduct of a sexual nature is considered harassment if it has the purpose or effect of substantially interfering with an individual's work environment or creates an intimidating, hostile, or offensive work environment.

Companies can protect themselves from charges of sexual harassment by clearly notifying all employees that such behavior will not be tolerated and by establishing and publicizing a procedure for dealing with complaints. A senior executive should administer this policy and all complaints should be quickly investigated and, if verified, quickly corrected.

Would assume that most people have sufficient common sense to refrain from making explicit sexual demands on fellow workers, and most do. That's why sexual harassers of their subordinates use much more subtle tactics. He or she may make a comment to the effect that other employees have benefited by being "more friendly." In the alternative, he or she may remark on a person's physical attributes or attire. These comments can be interpreted as harassment.

Does that mean that any compliment given to a member of the opposite sex could be construed as harassment? It depends on what you say and how you say it. A comment such as, "That's an attractive dress," is much different from the comment, "That dress is sexy." The statement "I like your new hairdo" is also acceptable, but the statement "Wearing your hair like that excites me," is not.

Take Randy, for example. He's a "toucher." When he greets people, he grasps their hands, pats them on the back and gives them hugs. That's his way of expressing himself and he's been doing it for years. He also is a kisser. He doesn't kiss his male associates, but when he greets his female colleagues, he often pecks them on the cheek. Randy was shocked when he was called into the human resources office and told that some of the women in his department had complained about his hugging and kissing. In Randy's eyes, these acts were acts of friendship with no sexual intent, but to the women who complained, they were unwelcome.

> *Toxic language creates a hostile work environment, and that's now illegal . . . Just as sexual harassment was ruled by the courts to create a hostile work environment so toxic language poses similar legal liabilities. Companies are being sued today for the language used by bosses.*
>
> Art Bell, TV Commentator

An Intimidating, Hostile, Work Environment

As noted earlier, according to its legal definition, sexual harassment includes conduct that creates an "intimidating and hostile work environment."

Ken's team, for example, had always been all-male and when two women were added to his group some of the men resented this "intrusion" on their masculine camaraderie. They made life unpleasant for the female team members by making snide remarks and by giving them incorrect information that caused them to make errors in their work. They excluded them from work-related discussions. Although, their actions can't be interpreted as "sexual" in nature, these behaviors still qualify as harassment. The men created a hostile work environment for the women.

Tina works in a warehouse and the off-color language some of the men continually use offends her. When she complains, she is told, "That's the way these guys talk. They talked this way before women worked here and they're not going to change now. Get used to it."

Because people may find that this dubious language creates "an offensive work environment," it can be legal grounds for a complaint. And note that the language need not be spoken. A hostile work environment can be created by "funny" e-mails of an off-color nature that are circulated around an office. If you receive such an e-mail, you should immediately let the sender know that such messages are inappropriate and will not be tolerated.

To an amazing extent, careless e-mailing has become one of the most frequent minefields in civil and criminal discovery. Case after case, ranging from criminal prosecutions to sexual harassment lawsuits, have been anchored on careless e-mails.

Kendall Coffey, Attorney

Managing Harassment on the Job

If you face off-color language in the workplace, your first move should be to talk to the people (or person) using the inappropriate language. Point out diplomatically that this behavior is unprofessional and offensive to both women and men and that it isn't appropriate to use to use such language in a business environment. Inform the offender(s) that such behavior can cause legal problems for the company and for them as individuals. Tell them that if they continue to use street language they will be subject to the same type of disciplinary action as is applicable to the violation of other company work rules.

Harassment Off-Site

It is a company's responsibility to manage sexual harassment that is connected with job-based relationships or situations, even if the harassment itself occurs outside the workplace. Cathy was perplexed. Dennis, one of the men in her department, had gone out a few times with Diane, who worked in another department. It never developed into a romance, but Diane kept bugging Dennis to go out with her again. Diane came into Dennis's office several times a day to talk with him, even though Dennis didn't welcome her visits. Diane's constant attention interfered with his work and he wasn't interested in seeing her. The next time Diane visited Dennis, Cathy called her aside and told her that such social visits were not permissible. Diane never returned, but continued to harass Dennis by telephoning him after work.

Even though the harassment had ceased at the job, because both Dennis and Diane were employed by the same company, the company had an obligation to stop Diane from bothering Dennis. Cathy should discuss the situation with Diane's manager and if necessary, with the human resources department. If Diane continued her harassment, appropriate disciplinary action would be necessary.

Sexual Harassment By Non-employees

Suppose that a salesperson who comes into the office makes a point of telling off-color jokes to the women who work there. Some of them think that he's hilarious, but you notice the look of disgust on the faces of others. Although no complaints have been made, you see that the behavior is creating an offensive work environment. The salesperson doesn't work for your company, but you still have an obligation to do something about it.

An employer is responsible for the offensive behavior of all its employees (regardless of whether they're in management) and even non-employees when the employer or its agents (that's us, in this case) know about it or should have known about it.

If we know about such behavior, we must speak to the person concerned, and tell him or her to discuss the matter with the sales rep. If the undesirable behavior continues, the company has an obligation to tell the salesperson that it cannot continue doing business with him.

Note that your company is responsible not only when it knows about the offensive behavior but also *when it should have known* about it. This point is a delicate one. How are you supposed to know about everything that might happen? You can't, of course, but if you're observant, you'd know a great deal about what transpires. In the preceding example, if you knew that the visiting sales rep had a propensity to use off-color language and tell provocative jokes when he took you out to lunch, you should know that he may also do so when speaking with other staff members.

Ten Steps to Prevent Sexual Harassment Charges

To prevent problems for yourself, your coworkers and the company itself, every organization should:

1. Establish a formal policy prohibiting sexual harassment. Clearly indicate any and all actions that could be construed as harassment and specify what steps employees should take if they are harassed. Appoint a senior executive to administer the policy.
2. Publicize the policy through bulletins, articles in the company newspaper, regularly scheduled meetings and training programs.
3. Make it easy for complainants to bring matters to the attention of management. Post notices throughout the office detailing who to go to and how to do it. Make sure that all employees know that there will be no retaliation against persons bringing complaints against anybody in the organization, regardless of rank or position.
4. Investigate all complaints—no matter how trivial or

unjustified they appear to you. Keep written records of all findings (including memos, reports of interviews, and statements from the complainant, the person accused and witnesses).

5. Never terminate or threaten complainants or potential complainants.
6. Don't make rash decisions. Analyze all the facts. Consult an attorney, as the matter may wind up in court.
7. Take action. If the complaint is justified, correct the situation. Depending on the case, this may include requiring the harasser to apologize, ordering a cessation of the acts that led to the complaint, adjusting the harasser's salary, promoting or changing the working conditions of the persons who have suffered or for flagrant or repeated offenses, firing the harasser.
8. If the investigation finds the complaint was not justified, explain the decision carefully and diplomatically to the complainant. Keep in mind that if he or she is not satisfied, a charge can still be filed with appropriate government agencies or brought to court.
9. Don't look for easy ways out. Transferring the harasser to another department may solve the immediate problem, but if the harasser repeats the offense in the new assignment, the situation is compounded.
10. If a formal complaint is made to the EEOC or an equivalent state agency, even if you feel the complaint is groundless, treat it seriously.

By following these ten guidelines, not only will you reduce the chances of having sexual harassment charges filed against the company, but you will also improve employees' morale, as they will see that you take this situation seriously.

Related Employees and Gender Discrimination

Some companies, fearing that closely related people working together will lead to complications, may prohibit parents, children, siblings and spouses from working in the same department or in positions in which they must interrelate.

Some states prohibit employers from discriminating against people who are married to each other, but these laws do not cover relationships other than spousal relationships and companies are left to deal with them at their own discretion. When it comes to marriage, additional complexities are possible. If a company prohibits married couples from working together and two team members marry, which one should leave the team? Some companies base their policy on rank (the lower-ranking spouse leaves) or salary (the lower-paid spouse leaves). However, because it may be more likely for the man to be the more highly ranked or highly paid employee, such a policy discriminates against women. The best way to deal with this issue is to let the couple make the determination about which one will leave the team or the organization.

Dealing with Generational Differences

Today's workforce may be comprised of as many as four generations working side by side and connecting with each other may present a challenge. Each generation has its own unique mindset, work style and ways of communicating. Accordingly, working and communicating across generations has become vital to building a cohesive, productive and successful team.

Now let's study the special problems that you face when interacting with different generations. As you learn to connect and communicate more effectively with one another, differences can be viewed as healthy and provide exciting opportunities to collaborate on innovative problem-solving.

> *Bridging the generation gap comes down to two simple ideas: understanding and respecting differences and learning how to communicate effectively.*
>
> Ken Owens

Criteria for Successful Cross-Generational Relationships

Sometimes the different outlooks on work and life by members of different generational groups seem to make the relationships difficult. Here are some suggestions to help you overcome these perceptions:

- Be truly interested in generational differences. Learn what generations outside of our own think about matters that concern all of us.
- Avoid holding grudges from clashes with people from other generations.
- Focus attention on our thoughts, feelings and behavior.
- Know your own generation. Recognize how our perception affects your encounters.
- Have positive feelings toward generations different from ours.
- Be aware of the impact of your behavior on other generations.

Certain attitudes, principles and concepts must be understood and performed consistently to ensure success and effectiveness in dealing with people who are different from us.

Contemporary Generations

Each generation has its own distinct set of values that developed from the social environment of its formative years. Different generations have different mores and beliefs regarding family, career, the work/life balance, training and development, loyalty, gender roles, the work environment and expectations of leaders. Demographers have named the different generations in the work force as Veterans, Baby Boomers, Generation X, and Generation Y.

Not everyone agrees on when each generation started, but the dates given below are generally reflected by most of the literature. In looking at these categories, you must be careful to avoid stereotyping and recognize that the characteristics provided are generalizations; all individuals have their own unique experiences and manifest their own personalites, which may or may not fit that of their generational cohorts.

Characteristics of Veterans

Veterans are people who were born prior to 1946. Their lives were affected by the Great Depression of the 1930s and World War II from 1939 to 1945. They tend to be disciplined, to respect law and order and to like consistency. This generation is not comfortable with change. They have fixed views on the role of each gender and in the workplace they are comfortable with a direct, command-andcontrol management style. Most Veterans are now retired, but there are a good number who are still employed, most often reporting to younger men and women.

Characteristics of the Baby Boomers Generation

The Baby Boomers were born between 1946 and 1964 and have the largest population of any generation. In their youth, they were open-minded and rebellious but became more conservative in their thirties and forties. Job status and social standing are important to this generation, who tend to be optimistic, ambitious and loyal. Many believe that employment is "for life." They created the concepts of the "workaholic" and the "superwoman."

Characteristics of Generation X

Gen X was born between 1965 and 1979. They were often raised by two working parents, were exposed to daycare and divorce, and became known as "latchkey kids." They are a well-educated generation with many members having tertiary qualifications and they are resourceful, individualistic, self-reliant and skeptical of authority. Unlike the Baby Boomers, they do not expect to have long-term careers with one employer, they do not expect to benefit from corporate loyalty and they are not interested in status symbols.

In the workplace, they focus on relationships, outcomes, their rights and their skills. They tend to change employment and even careers frequently and will leave a job if they are unhappy. They often have a "What's in it for me?" attitude. These are the men and women who at the time of this writing are set in and/or are advancing in their careers.

Characteristics of Generation Y

Gen Y (also know as the Net Generation and as the Millenials) was born between 1980 and 1995. They are very technology-savvy and are comfortable with ethnically diverse groups.

Their values are similar to those of Veterans in that they are optimistic, confident and sociable and they have strong morals and a sense of civic duty.

Members of Gen Y are not brand-loyal and the speed of the Internet has led the Net Generation to be flexible and changeable in its fashion and styleconsciousness. Those in this group have different practices and expectations about communication than members of other generations. They expect great workplace flexibility and are likely to change employers even more frequently than Gen Xers.

Their means of communication is mainly through online communities and social media like Twitter and Facebook rather than personally meeting their friends and developing relationships. They are capable of belonging to huge communities and having large-scale collaborations using the Internet without personally knowing the other group members. They may not perform well in areas such as public speaking.

Communication Tips for Connecting with Different Generations

Communicating with Veterans

- Keep them in the loop.
- Get to the point and don't waste their time.
- Use inclusive (i.e., "we, us") and more formal language to build trust.
- Keep them up-to-date on the company and the current projects and initiatives.
- Articulate how they can contribute to long-term strategic goals.

- For incentives, traditional rewards are often the best motivators.
- Use personal approaches versus e-mail, voice mail and faxes to communicate.
- Words are gospel. Make sure your words and body language are congruent.
- Don't expect them to share their thoughts until trust is built.

Communicating with Boomers

- Treat each individual as unique.
- Speak openly, frankly and directly.
- Give public recognition.
- Involve them in decisions and create a collaborative and consensual environment.
- Demonstrate flexibility.
- Appreciate their strong work ethic, willingness to work long hours and desire for opportunities to prove themselves.
- Speak in an open and direct style with plenty of body language.
- Answer questions frankly, thoroughly and expect to be pressed for details.
- Do not use controlling, manipulative language.
- Ask for or provide options to demonstrate flexibility in your thinking.
- Use face-to-face or electronic communication.

Communicating with Gen X

- Give them the elbow room to be creative in the way in which they accomplish their tasks and goals.

- Let them handle multiple projects and empower them to prioritize these projects themselves so they feel in control.
- Allow for opportunities for them to learn new skills and provide a variety of responsibilities.
- Use constructive and direct feedback in their language.
- Make them feel like insiders by sharing information.
- Listen attentively and respect their opinions.
- Be brief and concise to hold their attention.
- Use a direct style to present the facts.
- Challenge them and ask them for their input.
- Share information with them immediately and often.
- Use an informal communication style.
- Listen and show respect for their opinion.
- Use e-mail as a primary communication tool.

Communicating with Gen Y

- Let words paint visual pictures to inspire, motivate and keep them focused.
- Don't be condescending; show respect through your language.
- Make a practice of constantly seeking their feedback.
- Use humor.
- Encourage them to think outside the box and challenge them to explore new paths or options.
- Help them to understand the personal benefits of a task or goal.
- Focus on their personal goals and try to weave them into the job.
- Provide them with opportunities that will enhance their personal growth, power and responsibility.

- Delegate challenging, meaningful work to them and make sure that they understand how it leads toward meeting company or department objectives.
- Show respect and provide an environment where reciprocal feedback is sought.
- Encourage them to think outside the box.
- Use e-mail, texting, instant messaging and voicemail as primary communication tools.

Nobody grows old merely by living a number of years. We grow old by deserting our ideals. Years may wrinkle the skin, but to give up enthusiasm wrinkles the soul.

Samuel Ullman

Messages that Motivate the Generations

Regardless of one's generation, everyone thrives on sincere appreciation, praise and recognition. You need to give appreciation that is meaningful to members of a particular group, or it will be viewed as insincere. By identifying traits or values that are important to individuals and letting them know, in their terms, how their efforts have affected others based on what they value, messages of gratitude will make a huge impact. Here are some suggestions on accomplishing this:

1. Tell staff members exactly what you admire. Be specific. Instead of saying, "Your work was good," say, "The program you designed was a major factor in our successful completion of the project."
2. Explain why you expressed your gratitude for the specific effort and the evidence you have to support it. (This gives

your appreciation credibility and distinguishes it from flattery.) "The reason I say that is. . . ."

3. Ask a question about the person's contribution or approach to the achievement at issue. Doing so will get him or her talking and encourage interaction.

> *Leaders who understand the conditions that shaped each generation and the values and beliefs that flowed from those conditions, will have a handy set of tools in creating strong relationships and teams for getting things done.*
>
> Ken Owens, Tellabs

Misconceptions in Thinking Among the Generations

- Everybody is the same—not everyone wants to give it all to the organization.
- Everybody wants the same thing out of work—not everyone shares the drive for power, status and money.
- Everybody wants to be promoted—many people seek recognition rather than promotion.
- Everybody wants to be a manager—many talented employees have no desire to be managers.
- Everybody wants to live up to the expectations.

Every generation is alike in that they want to be paid fairly and to be shown respect. Yet, each generation responds to different managerial practices and leadership approaches.

Delivering Constructive Feedback

Delivering criticism or feedback that can be heard, accepted and acted upon is an essential skill for successfully managing people across generations. Research shows that improvements in productivity depend upon accurate and relevant feedback delivered constructively. Yet, most people deliver feedback the same way across the board and fail to connect with the individual. The bottom line is that constructive feedback leads to improvement in performance. The challenge is learning how to deliver it in a way that will be incorporated into the employee's work.

> *Father Time is not always a hard parent, and though he tarries for none of his children, often lays his hand lightly upon those who have used him well; making them old men and women inexorably enough, but leaving their hearts and spirits young and in full vigour. With such people the grey head is but the impression of the old fellow's hand in giving them his blessing and every wrinkle but a notch in the quiet calendar of a well-spent life.*
>
> Charles Dickens

Targeting Feedback to Each Generation

Research suggests that different generations view feedback in different ways:

- *Veterans*: "No news is good news." Veterans don't seek or expect feedback, but appreciate acknowledgment that they have made a difference.
- *Boomers*: "Feedback once a year and put it in writing." Boomers don't expect feedback, particularly positive feedback, except for an annual review.

- *Gen-Xers*: "Sorry to interrupt, but how am I doing?" Gen-Xers need feedback to assure them that they are on the right track and to stay motivated.
- *Gen-Yers*: "Feedback when I want it at the push of a button." Those of the Gen-Y group are used to continuous feedback, input and praise. They need to know what they are doing and if it's right or wrong.

Managing Older Staff Members

Younger supervisors and managers are often concerned about how their older subordinates feel about being supervised by someone who is younger and often less experienced than they are. The most important thing to know is that most people will take their cues from you as leaders. If you seem hesitant or are obviously concerned about the age difference, people will notice it and it will become a concern for them too. If we act like it's a nonissue, it will quickly become a nonissue to most (or with luck, all) of the people. So the key is getting yourself into a frame of mind where you genuinely believe that your age is a nonissue and where you're comfortable with your authority.

You should also think about how you present yourself. You should avoid using language, mannerisms, or a tone of voice that unintentionally gives off an aura of "I'm young, inexperienced or lack confidence." You must show by your actions that you are able to solicit other people's input but are comfortable making a decision of your own at the end of that process. You must learn to give feedback without sounding nervous or apologetic.

You should make a concerted effort from the start to educate yourself about how to manage well, how to delegate well, how to give feedback, how to set goals and hold people accountable to them, how to handle performance problems, how to develop good workers and how to exercise authority without being either an unreasonable tyrant or a easy-going pushover.

> *Age is opportunity no less,*
> *Than youth itself, though in another dress, And as the evening twilight fades away, the sky is filled with stars, invisible by day.*
>
> Henry Wadsworth Longfellow

Retraining Older Workers

Can older workers be retrained to work with the constantly changing technologies of today? Many supervisors—and indeed, many workers themselves—believe older people cannot change their old work methods and cannot be developed into productive workers using new methods.

When Chelsea, a public relations department supervisor heard that they were replacing their electronic newsletters with website updates, she was terribly concerned. Some of her associates were young and could easily be trained to post the updates in HTML. But what about her older staff members, like Jeannette? She had been using the e-mail method for over ten years and she was fifty years old! Chelsea worried that Jeannette and some of her other associates couldn't learn something as complicated as HTML. Everybody knows "you can't teach an old dog new tricks."

Chelsea's way of thinking has caused an enormous amount of anxiety for older people and their supervisors. The idea that there is an age limit to the ability to learn is totally absurd. People of any age can learn—if they have the basic intelligence and the desire to do so. (Note that older people themselves are often concerned about their ability to learn new methods or approaches. With some frequency, Chelsea's type of concern is shared by people like Jeannette, who believe that they won't be able to learn to use new technology. Until this attitude is overcome, it is very unlikely that such older workers will be trained successfully.)

A recent study conducted by the American Association of Retired People brought out that managers at most companies are concerned about the older workers' ability to keep up with the changes and developments in their fields, but most companies do little about it. While 55 percent of the individuals believed training would be effective for older workers, only 29 percent of them offered such training programs.

One company that does train older people is General Electric. This company reported that in one of its facilities, it annually trains about 1,100 engineers and technicians in new technology and about one-third of these trainees are over fifty years old. Some take courses right up to their retirement.

Some company managers are concerned with the cost of broad staff training. Why bother training older workers when they will retire in a few years? This attitude is shortsighted. The increase in a person's capability and productivity, even for a few years, usually justifies the cost of such training. Not only is the older worker stimulated, but younger employees see that the company is concerned with all of its staff members, and as they get on in years, they will also be continually trained and valued.

Build Self-Confidence in Older Workers

How did Jeannette feel? She has been one of the best public relations writers in the company. She prided herself on this accomplishment. Now, her main task is being taken from her. She will have to learn a completely new program. And as everybody knows, the web is for young people.

In order to get Jeannette started properly, it is necessary to help her overcome this fear. The other associates had always looked up to her, and now they will be more skilled than she.

The supervisor and others involved in the training must recognize Jeannette's situation and make a special effort to build up her self-confidence. Before the training starts, they should spend time with Jeannette discussing how the training will be done. Learn what her main worries are. Reinforce the concept that older people can learn by giving her examples of several people in her age group who have mastered using HTML easily. She should be assured of your confidence in her ability. To do this you should point out the similarities between the old method and the new. Indicate that the training is done in a positive manner. Nothing will be done to embarrass her. Above all, you must be patient and not give up or let her give up on herself easily.

Coach

You should act as a coach—not like a schoolmaster, who lectures, grades assignments, and passes or fails the student. Like the good coach of an athletic team, you should demonstrate, observe and comment, give pep talks and acknowledge every improvement.

Mentors

Often one of the trainee's coworkers can be more successful than the supervisor in assisting the training process. Despite the efforts of Chelsea to overcome Jeannette's resistance to learning, she did not succeed until one of Jeanette's friends interceded.

Michelle, another public relations associate, was not much younger than Jeannette. She never had a doubt that she could learn to use the computer and was one of the first people in the department to do so. Chelsea asked Michelle to be Jeannette's mentor. Michelle convinced Jeannette that if she, at her age, could learn to use HTML, there was no reason Jeannette couldn't. By constant encouragement, by her own example, by showing her little tricks that had helped her learn and most importantly, by never ceasing her support, she gradually helped Jeannette gain the self-confidence she needed.

Give Positive Reinforcement

Dale Carnegie said, "Praise the slightest improvement and praise each improvement. Be hearty in your approbation and lavish in your praise." B.F. Skinner, the famous behavioral psychologist, proved in his experiments that when people are praised for their successes instead of criticized for their faults, they will be more likely to succeed. By giving these older workers encouragement, support and praise for their achievements, they will succeed. They will also show their older coworkers that although we may not be able to teach an old dog new tricks, it is certainly not true of humans.

Sum and Substance

- Sexual harassment is not limited to demands for sexual favors. It also includes permitting the creation of a work environment that is hostile or offensive to employees because of their gender.
- Make all employees aware of the policy prohibiting sexual harassment and specify steps to be taken to bring it to management's attention.
- Managers can be held liable for sexual harassment in their departments not only if they know about it and fail to take action, but even if they did not know about it, if they reasonably should have known.
- Be vigilant. Follow the ten steps to prevent sexual harassment charges that are listed in this chapter.
- Today's workforce may be comprised of as many as four generations working side by side and connecting with each other may present a challenge.
- Demographers have named the different generations in the work force as Veterans (born before 1945), Baby Boomers (1946-1964), Generation X (1965-1979), and Generation Y (1980-1995).
- You must be careful to avoid stereotyping and recognize that although, the characteristics of each generation listed in this chapter are generalizations, each individual manifests his or her own personality, which may or may not align with the personalities of his or her generational cohorts.
- Reread the communication tips in this chapter to effectively communicate with each generational group. You must understand how they act and react to what you say.

- Do not assume that members of a generation different from yours think the way you do. Listen, observe and interact with them to clarify what motivates them and what turns them off.
- Improvements in productivity depend upon accurate, relevant feedback delivered constructively. The challenge is learning how to deliver it in a manner that is adapted to each generation's preferred communication style.
- Younger supervisors and managers are often concerned about how their older subordinates feel about being supervised by them. You should avoid using language, mannerisms or a tone of voice that unintentionally communicates that, "I'm young, inexperienced or lack confidence." You must show by our actions that you are able to solicit other people's input but are comfortable making a decision of your own. You must learn to give feedback without sounding nervous or apologetic.
- Older workers can be retrained. By giving them encouragement, support and praise for their achievements, they will succeed and serve as an example to other older coworkers.

Appendix A

ABOUT DALE CARNEGIE

Dale Carnegie was a pioneer in what is now referred to as the human potential movement. His teachings and writings have helped people all over the world become self-confident, personable and influential individuals.

In 1912, Carnegie offered his first course in public speaking at a YMCA in New York City. As in most public speaking courses given at that time, Carnegie started the class with a theoretical lecture but quickly noticed that the class members looked bored and restless. Something had to be done.

Dale stopped his lecture and calmly pointed to a man in the back row and asked him to get up and give an impromptu talk about his background. When the student finished, he asked another student to speak about himself and so on until everybody in the class had given a brief talk. With the encouragement of their classmates and guidance from Carnegie, each of them overcame their fright and gave satisfactory talks.

"Without knowing what I was doing," Carnegie later reported, "I stumbled on the best method of conquering fear."

His course became so popular that he was asked to give it in other cities. As the years went by, he kept improving the content of the course. He learned that the students were most interested in increasing their self-confidence, improving their interpersonal relations, becoming successful in their careers and overcoming fear and worry. This resulted in the emphasis of the course being shifted from public speaking to dealing with these matters. The talks became the means to an end rather than the end itself.

In addition to what he learned from his students, Carnegie engaged in extensive research on the approach to life of successful men and women. He incorporated this into his classes. This led to the writing of his most famous book, "*How To Win Friends and Influence People*."

This book became an instant best seller and since its publication in 1936 (and its revised edition in 1981), over 20 million copies have been sold. It has been translated into 36 languages. In 2002, *How to Win Friends and Influence People* was named the #1 Business Book of the 20th Century. In 2008, Fortune Magazine listed it as one of the seven books every leader should have in his or her bookcase. His book, *How To Stop Worrying and Start Living*, written in 1948 has also sold millions of copies and has been translated into 27 languages.

Dale Carnegie died on November 1, 1955. An obituary in a Washington newspaper summed up his contribution to society:

> *"Dale Carnegie solved none of the profound mysteries of the universe. But, perhaps, more than anyone of his generation, he helped human beings learn how to get along together—which seems sometimes to be the greatest need of all."*

About Dale Carnegie & Associates, Inc.

Founded in 1912, Dale Carnegie Training has evolved from one man's belief in the power of self-improvement to a performance-based training company with offices worldwide. It focuses on giving people in business the opportunity to sharpen their skills and improve their performance in order to build positive, steady and profitable results.

Dale Carnegie's original body of knowledge has been constantly updated, expanded and refined through nearly a century's worth of real-life business experiences. The 160 Dale Carnegie Franchisees around the world use their training and consulting services with companies of all sizes in all business segments to increase knowledge and performance. The result of this collective, global experience is an expanding reservoir of business acumen that our clients rely on to get business results.

Headquartered in Hauppauge, New York, Dale Carnegie Training is represented in all 50 of the United States and over 75 countries. More than 2,700 instructors present Dale Carnegie Training programs in more than 25 languages. Dale Carnegie Training is dedicated to serving the business community worldwide. In fact, approximately 7 million people have completed Dale Carnegie Training.

Dale Carnegie Training emphasizes practical principles and processes by designing programs that offer people the knowledge, skills and practices they need to add value to the business. Connecting proven solutions with real-world challenges, Dale Carnegie Training is recognized internationally as the leader in bringing out the best in people.

Among the graduates of these programs are CEOs of major corporations, owners and managers of businesses of every size and every commercial and industrial activity, legislative and executive leaders of governments and countless individuals whose lives have been enriched by the experience.

In an ongoing global survey on customer satisfaction, 99 percent of Dale Carnegie Training graduates express satisfaction with the training they receive.

Appendix B

DALE CARNEGIE'S PRINCIPLES

Become a Friendlier Person

1. Don't criticize, condemn or complain.
2. Give honest, sincere appreciation.
3. Arouse in the other person an eager want.
4. Become genuinely interested in other people.
5. Smile.
6. Remember that a person's name is to that person the sweetest sound in any language.
7. Be a good listener. Encourage others to talk about themselves.
8. Talk in terms of the other person's interests.
9. Make the other person feel important—and do it sincerely.
10. To get the best of an argument—avoid it.
11. Show respect for the other person's opinion. Never tell a person he or she is wrong.
12. If you are wrong, admit it quickly, emphatically.
13. Begin in a friendly way.

14. Get the other person saying "yes" immediately.
15. Let the other person do a great deal of the talking.
16. Let the other person feel the idea is his or hers.
17. Try honestly to see things from the other person's point of view.
18. Be sympathetic with the other person's ideas and desires.
19. Appeal to the nobler motives.
20. Dramatize your ideas.
21. Throw down a challenge.
22. Begin with praise and honest appreciation.
23. Call attention to people's mistakes indirectly.
24. Talk about your own mistakes before criticizing the other person.
25. Ask questions instead of giving direct orders.
26. Let the other person save face.
27. Praise the slightest improvement and praise every improvement. Be "hearty in your approbation and lavish in your praise."
28. Give the other person a fine reputation to live up to.
29. Use encouragement. Make the fault seem easy to correct.
30. Make the other person happy about doing the thing you suggest.

Fundamental Principles for Overcoming Worry

1. Live in "day-tight compartments."
2. How to face trouble:
3. Ask yourself, "What is the worst that can possibly happen?"
4. Prepare to accept the worst.
5. Try to improve on the worst.
6. Remind yourself of the exorbitant price you can pay for worry in terms of your health.

Basic Techniques in Analyzing Worry

1. Get all the facts.
2. Weigh all the facts—then come to a decision.
3. Once a decision is reached, act!
4. Write out and answer the following questions:
    - What is the problem?
    - What are the causes of the problem?
    - What are the possible solutions?
    - What is the best possible solution?

Break the Worry Habit Before It Breaks You

1. Keep busy.
2. Don't fuss about trifles.
3. Use the law of averages to outlaw your worries.
4. Cooperate with the inevitable.
5. Decide just how much anxiety a thing may be worth and refuse to give it more.
6. Don't worry about the past.

Cultivate a Mental Attitude That Will Bring You Peace and Happiness

1. Fill your mind with thoughts of peace, courage, health and hope.
2. Never try to get even with your enemies.
3. Expect ingratitude.
4. Count your blessings—not your troubles.
5. Do not imitate others.
6. Try to profit from your losses.
7. Create happiness for others.